Energy Efficient Affordable Housing

Sasha Tsenkova

Energy Efficient Affordable Housing

Policy Design and Implementation in Canadian Cities

Springer

Sasha Tsenkova
School of Architecture, Planning and Landscape
University of Calgary
Calgary, AB, Canada

ISBN 978-3-030-69562-0 ISBN 978-3-030-69563-7 (eBook)
https://doi.org/10.1007/978-3-030-69563-7

This Springer imprint is published by the registered company Springer Nature Switzerland AG.
The registered company address is: Gewerbestrasse 11, 6330 Cham, Switzerland

Acknowledgements

The book provides the first comprehensive evaluation of decade-long energy efficiency retrofit programs in the affordable housing sector of Canadian cities. It situates this comparative assessment in a theoretical framework focused on policy design with links to key policy instruments—regulatory, financial, and institutional—in relation to major results achieved. The approach is interdisciplinary, supported by rich empirical data from case studies, observations, and interviews.

The book systematically presents the results of affordable housing energy efficiency initiatives in Toronto, Vancouver, Edmonton, and Calgary. The research is developed with a sense of urgency as the quest for transformational change of social and affordable housing will be the focus of many public programs and strategies for economic and social recovery in twenty-first century cities. Affordable housing has become of paramount importance in the context of the COVID-19 pandemic, underscoring its significance for public health and urban resilience. Energy-efficient retrofits respond to environmental and social imperatives and set the stage for partnerships with the public, private, and not-for-profit providers in the social housing sector. This book offers valuable lessons for the design, planning, and implementation of energy retrofit programs in Canada and beyond.

It was a pleasure to collaborate with many individuals during the research process. My research assistants—Cheryl Cliff, Chelsea Whitty, and Karim Youssef—were very dedicated and thoughtful contributors to the analysis of city-wide retrofit initiatives and case study projects. Jeremy Tran made an exceptional contribution to the evaluation of the new wave of programs. I do appreciate his professionalism and attention to detail. My special thanks to many individuals who shared their views on program implementation in Toronto, Vancouver, Calgary, and Edmonton. The insights of many policymakers—federal, provincial, municipal—social housing providers, engineers, planners, and program managers were instrumental in shaping the comparative research process. I am very grateful for their efforts, dedication, and candid responses. I would like to acknowledge the specific contribution of Arlene Rawson and Phil Fan from Shelter, Support & Housing Administration at the City of Toronto who were dedicated advisors and enthusiastic supporters of this research over the years. I was fortunate to cooperate with Dr Johannes Glaeser and Judith Kripp who were very professional sponsoring editors at Springer in Heidelberg, Germany.

The research was supported by grants from Canada School of Energy and the Environment and the Social Sciences and Humanities Research Council of Canada. I hope that the book will inspire future coherent efforts and investment in sustainable energy retrofits to improve affordable housing while creating green jobs and benefiting the environment. In the context of post-pandemic economic recovery, there is an excellent opportunity to invest in a greener and more inclusive urban future.

Sasha Tsenkova

Contents

List of Figures

List of Tables

List of Boxes

Chapter 1
Energy Efficiency Retrofits and Policy Design for Sustainable Affordable Housing

1.1 The Need for Transformative Change in Social Housing

Rethinking the role of social and affordable housing is of great importance to society and to our cities, where over 60% of the people live and work, particularly given the rapid growth of urban poverty and vulnerability. Comparative studies indicate a renewed emphasis on the supply of social housing and city-wide initiatives to encourage private and not-for-profit provision to build new mixed income communities. Such initiatives in European and North American cities are complimented by investment in existing affordable housing to improve its quality and energy performance, often benefiting from environmental subsidy programs responding to climate change imperatives. Access to affordable housing in cities has become of paramount importance in the context of COVID-19 pandemic, underscoring its significance for public health and urban resilience. Housing is providing a safe refuge from the outside world, while serving as a place for productive work, advancement in education and family interaction. The quest for transformational change of social and affordable housing in the future will be the focus of many public programs and strategies for economic and social recovery in twenty-first century cities. *The European Union Renovation Wave*, initiated by the European Commission tackles energy poverty and worst-performing buildings. A new *Affordable Housing Initiative* for renovation and retrofits sets the stage for collaboration across the EU and provides blueprints for scaling up of program results. Other countries see this as an integral part of a green economic post-pandemic recovery.

Reviews of existing practices of energy efficiency retrofits in affordable housing indicate that countries with a strong social housing legacy have introduced a range of policy instruments and economic stimulus packages to develop an energy portfolio framework synergistic with existing social housing asset management (Milin and Bullier 2011; Peuportier et al. 2007). In countries with a higher share of social housing, managed by not-for-profit providers on a cost recovery basis, social and affordable housing is regarded as an important sector to mobilize municipal,

S. Tsenkova, *Energy Efficient Affordable Housing*,
https://doi.org/10.1007/978-3-030-69563-7_1

provincial and national efforts to reduce energy consumption and GHG emissions (van Bortel et al. 2019). Engaging with the social and affordable housing sector on energy sustainability over the last decade has provided tangible economic, social and environmental benefits (Morrison 2013). Social housing providers, supported through a variety of regulatory, fiscal and financial policy instruments, have taken the lead in sustainable retrofits and some innovative entrepreneurial models have emerged in the Netherlands, Austria, Sweden and Germany (Bardhan et al. 2012; Housing Europe 2019). The social and affordable housing sector has the capacity for directing public investments towards generating public benefits for people. Energy sustainability retrofits help housing providers lower their energy use and energy bills, which reduces their long-term dependence on public funding. Lower operational costs allow property managers to allocate resources towards preventative maintenance and regular property rehabilitation. The investment in green and affordable housing creates jobs and improves the quality of life of social housing tenants, potentially leading to greater satisfaction with housing services.

In countries with a smaller social housing sector (usually less than 5%), the process is more fragmented and the impact of current practices on energy retrofits in social and affordable housing limited due to 'stop-and-go' funding and lack of institutional capacity. While there is a growing commitment to energy retrofits of social housing in the political rhetoric, few countries with a small social housing sector have moved forward in a strategic way (Centrum für Energietechnologie 2008). Rental units are often rented to low-income households, the stock is older with high energy intensity and poor insulation occupied by energy poor vulnerable households (Rowlands and Stephen 2016). Despite the capacity of social housing providers in housing management, the practice of energy efficiency retrofits often resolves to 'low-hanging fruit' opportunities (Weber 1997). This book aims at addressing a significant gap in the existing research by focusing on strategies of housing providers in the social and affordable housing in Canada. Despite its small share, the sector has the potential to deliver quality and energy efficiency improvements through large-scale public investment. Social housing providers share similarities in governance, institutional assets, capacities and regulations, allowing more efficient and effective program implementation (Toronto and Region Conservation Authority 2017). This presents a greater opportunity to concentrate large scale public funding and investment that will reach a large number of dwellings and achieve significant GHG/energy savings (Jenkins 2010; Office of Energy Efficiency 2009). However, the barriers for systematic adoption of energy retrofits as an integral part of the asset management strategy are more significant, limiting the potential for transformative change.

1.2 Research Objectives

This research responds to global and local imperatives for reducing the energy consumption through sustainable refurbishment of existing housing. Energy savings in the built environment have a high priority due to their potential to improve the security of the energy supply, reduce greenhouse gas (GHG) emissions and respond to climate change imperatives (Engelund and Wittchen 2008; Itard and Klunder 2007). In Canada, housing accounts for 17% of secondary energy use and 16% of GHG emissions, with over 80% of residential energy use related to space and hot water heating (Natural Resources Canada 2006). Within this context, sustainable transformation of existing housing constitutes an extensive societal challenge and is of great importance for the reduction of environmental impacts caused by the use of non-renewable energy sources (Hamilton et al. 2010; Fuller 2009). The federal government in partnership with provincial governments and territories launched policy initiatives supporting energy efficiency social housing retrofits in an effort to create green jobs and provide an efficient response to climate change. Within the context of this political commitment during the last decade, this research focuses on the following objectives:

- To review national and provincial policies and programs to implement energy efficiency retrofits in social housing;
- To identify preferred investment strategies and policy responses by different social housing providers—public, private non-profit and community (cooperative);
- To evaluate the results achieved in several domains: economic/financial, social, technical/technological and environmental through an in-depth analysis of select case studies;
- To synthesize lessons and develop a roadmap for future program design to achieve more strategic change in the social housing sector of Canadian cities.

The book provides the first comparative assessment of the energy-efficiency retrofit programs in the social housing sector of Canadian cities, focusing on program efficiency and effectiveness. The analytical framework explores key policy instruments—regulatory, fiscal and institutional—in relation to major results achieved. The approach is interdisciplinary, supported by rich empirical data from case studies, observations and interviews. The book explores important strategies for the provision of green and affordable housing, while addressing climate change imperatives and building resilience. Its value added contribution to scholarship is complemented by practical relevance for social housing organisations across Canada, but also for countries with a small residual housing sector. It offers valuable lessons for the design, planning and implementation of energy retrofit programs in North America and beyond.

The comparative research investigates the design and the implementation of energy efficiency programs in the housing sector with a particular focus on the investment decisions and choices made by social housing organisations. The geographic focus is limited to three provinces and four large cities where federal programs have been complemented by provincial and municipal ones since 2009. Such synergies are expected to generate more robust results and implementation practices, particularly in Toronto and Vancouver with a higher concentration of these types of innovative and experimental projects.

The research is exploratory in nature and is designed to provide the first systematic evaluation of energy efficiency residential programs in Canada using an interdisciplinary framework of analysis. The general hypothesis is that a more supportive policy framework for energy efficient transformation of social housing will yield better results (McKinsey and Company 2009). Furthermore, the institutional culture, market share, commitment to sustainability and ability to innovate of social housing providers will put them in a better position to implement innovative strategies for energy efficiency retrofits in their portfolio (Niebor et al. 2012; Pitt 2007). The main research questions are:

- What policy instruments support energy efficiency improvements in the social housing sector in British Colombia, Ontario and Alberta?
- How are these policies and programs implemented by different types of social housing providers?
- What types of energy efficient retrofits are the preferred choice, and why?

1.3 Theoretical and Analytical Framework

1.3.1 Housing Policy Design Continuum

Models of policy design and implementation provide an important theoretical departure for the analytical framework developed for this comparative research. As the literature suggests, models of policy decision-making where change is planned in advance differ radically from the ones which respond to contextual factors and politics (see Tsenkova 2003, 2009). Policy design is viewed as a process related to the 'policy life cycle'—policy formulation, choice of policy instruments, policy implementation, and monitoring/evaluation (Linder and Peters 1989). The two best known models of public policy decision-making are the rational model and the incremental model. Other models seek to combine rationality and incrementalism (Forrester 1984) or portray decision-making as a non-rational process based on convenience and power, such as the garbage can model (Cohen et al. 1972).

An idealized model of rational policy-making process consists of goal setting, analysis of all alternative strategies and a choice of the most efficient and effective alternative, but the practical implementation often faces political and institutional constraints. The incremental model of policy action through 'trial and error' offers concession to rational policy making, focusing on problems and complex relations between bureaucrats, politicians, and representatives of interest groups. The outcome does not imply fundamentally new approaches, but if consistently implemented over time may result in strategic change (Lindbloom 1979). This might seem 'sensible politics' because new options are not very different from present and past policies. However, in cases where 'trial and error' policy does not follow a particular strategic direction, but responds to challenges in the political environment and budget constraints, it becomes less effective and can be defined as

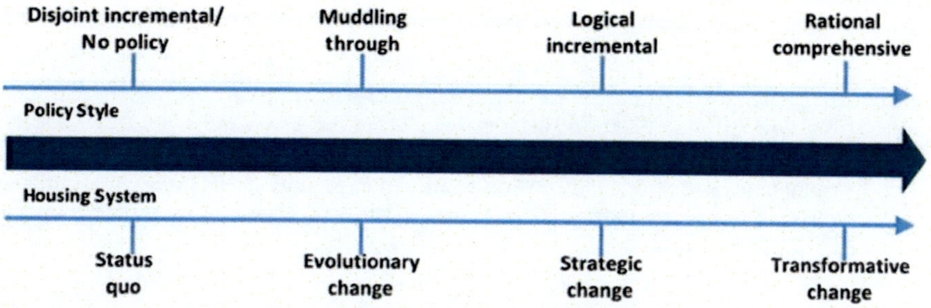

Fig. 1.1 Housing Policy Design Continuum. *Source: Author*

'muddling through' (Lindbloom 1979). Positive outcomes can be reversed over time due to lack of continuity and institutional commitment.

Correspondingly, at the other end of the spectrum is policy design where policy-makers do not necessarily work towards a set of planned changes in small steps, but rather leave the process to external factors—a style known as disjointed incrementalism (Lindblom 1977). Taken together, policy design/models of decision-making and the desirable outcomes define a policy continuum ranging from—status quo—evolutionary—strategic—transformational (see Fig. 1.1). Characterizing the policy outcomes and the degree of change in the housing system is important. For example, evolutionary change could be perceived as operational and policy intervention described as 'doing more of the same'. Strategic change implies shifting and redefining system requirements to achieve policy objectives, while transformation means a major departure from the status quo and commitment to a radical shift in policy (see Tsenkova 2003).

Different styles of policy-making influence the implementation process over time and the adjustment of strategies for intervention through appropriate choice of resources and policy instruments (Tsenkova 2009). Notwithstanding the diversity of arrangements, instruments can be grouped into the following categories: *voluntary* (community, non-profit, markets), *mixed* (information, subsidy, taxation) and *compulsory* (regulation and direct provision) (Schüle 2009; Thibert 2007).

1.3.2 Analytical Framework

The framework for analysis connects the policy design continuum with the application of network theory to comparative analysis of the operation of social housing actors (see Van Bortel and Elsinga 2007; Van Bortel and Mullins 2009). The emphasis is on mutually dependent actors—governments, social housing providers, resident associations, housing industry institutions—with none of them dominant in the process of policy formulation and implementation (Kickert et al. 1997; Lowndes and Skelcher 2002). The analytical framework applied to this research views the investment strategies of social housing providers as contextually dependent on the policy environment in which they operate. The policy environment is deconstructed through analysis of a range of policy instruments (regulatory, fiscal and financial) to determine the main factors affecting the types of retrofits implemented and investment priorities (Tsenkova 2018).

Furthermore, investment strategies are defined by the nature of social housing organisations operating between state, market and civil society. Brandsen et al. (2005) distinguish between state-led (public), market-led (private non-profit) and community-led housing organisations. Research indicates that state-led housing organisations, such as municipal providers, might be relatively easy for governments to influence to invest in the energy efficiency of their housing stock through bureaucratic mechanisms (Gruis and Nieboer 2004). Market and community-led organisations, however, may require different approaches—stimulation programmes including financial, regulatory and communicative measures—to be persuaded. Market-led, non-profit housing organisations are sensitive to the return on investment and could be reluctant to invest in the energy efficiency of their stock if it cannot be recovered by an increase in rental income (Gruis et al. 2009). In addition to position in the state-market-society triangle, other factors may influence the willingness and ability of organizations to invest in energy efficiency, such as the size, knowledge and skills within the organisation, available financial resources and the market position of its housing stock (Engelund and Wittchen 2008).

The analytical model employed in the research project centres on links between policy design, specific policy objectives, policy instruments—regulatory, fiscal and institutional—and implementation choices by social housing providers. The primary research explores investment decisions at the project level by different types of social housing organisations—public, private not-for-profit and cooperative. Programs under *Canada's Economic Action Plan*—managed by the provinces and by Canada Mortgage and Housing Corporation—are reviewed to capture important differences in their institutional model, funding criteria and results achieved (Tsenkova 2013, 2018). This is followed by a review of the new wave of programs and investment in the 2014–2020 period to illustrate differences and similarities of policy implementation at the provincial and municipal level.

At the project level, attention is paid to outcomes related to types of energy retrofits carried out, building envelope improvements, costs, energy savings and affordability (types of energy efficiency measures), financial risks and cost recovery (see Beerepoot 2007; Fuller 2009; Mlecnik et al. 2010). The profiling of these project-based outcomes is integrated in a broad comparative evaluation of CEAP program long-term results focused on efficiency and effectiveness. Given the small sample of case study projects, these conclusions utilise findings from the literature review, comments from key informants and personal observations. The efficiency of results is reviewed with reference to relevance of objectives, institutional arrangements and the quality of program design and implementation. The efficiency is particularly important as it evaluates the achievement of objectives with optimal use of resources and the overall impact over the social housing sector (see Tsenkova 2006). The effectiveness of energy retrofit programs in the social housing sector is

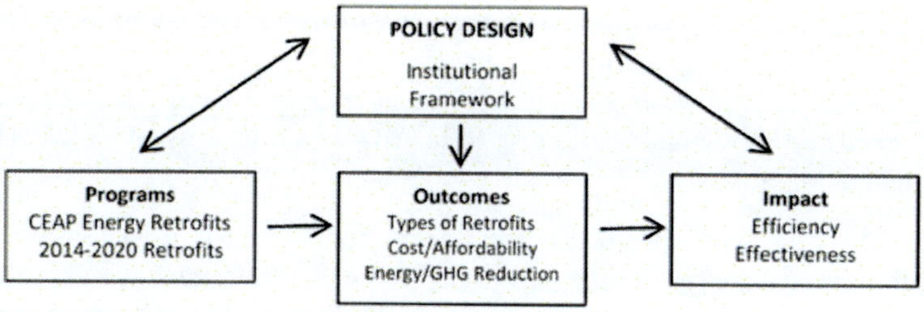

Fig. 1.2 Analytical framework. Source: Adapted from Tsenkova (2013)

reviewed with a reference to project achievements, quality of the retrofits and energy savings (Fig. 1.2).

1.4 Research Methodology

The research is structured in two parts, and employed both qualitative and quantitative techniques.

Review of the Literature First, policy instruments at the national and provincial level were explored more broadly through a review of the literature: monographs on social housing, officially published documents on energy efficiency policies, reports, and working paper series. This phase included the development of survey instruments and tools (templates) for comparative assessment of energy efficiency improvements in social housing.

Surveys and Field Work Second, the collection of quantitative indicators (time-series data) was carried out though a survey instrument administered with the assistance of experts from provincial umbrella organizations representing social housing providers. The set of housing and energy efficiency retrofit indicators in the survey tracked progress using time series data on social housing projects funded through the *Canada Economic Action Plan* at the provincial and city level organized in four blocks: (1) allocation of funds to public, non-profit and cooperative providers; (2) subsidies for energy efficient retrofits; (3) subsidies for building envelope and mechanical systems upgrades; and (4) basic program targets. The survey was administered by e-mail to provide a rapid assessment of the conditions in the social housing sector, market shares of different types of social providers, and access to funding to carry out energy efficiency projects. Up to 15 face-to-face interviews with housing policy experts (federal, provincial, municipal) complemented the assessment and were instrumental in compiling a typology of housing retrofit responses under the federal and provincial programs in Toronto, Vancouver, Calgary and

Edmonton.[1] This first phase of the primary research was essential for the selection of case study projects for in-depth evaluation and profiling. The same approach was consistently applied in 2019 to explore the range of energy retrofit programs at the federal and provincial level initiated in 2014 as a follow up of the CEAP and climate change initiatives.

The case study projects were selected on the basis of recommendations from program managers with the purpose of demonstrating innovative practices in energy efficiency upgrades and some of the more comprehensive measures implemented, including building envelope, technical system upgrades and installation of renewable energy sources. Data on investment strategies and policy responses by social housing providers was collected through primary research into 19 case studies to illustrate the diversity of experiences. The fieldwork during this second phase documented improvements in quality, technical and financial aspects, technology (types of energy efficiency measures), financial risks and cost recovery. Key informant interviews were undertaken with 25 housing policy makers, social housing providers, funding institutions, and municipal and/or provincial organizations with pertinent expertise and immediate involvement in the case study projects from March 2011 to December 2012. Follow up interviews related to the post CEAP programs were carried out from March to September 2019.

1.5 Organisation of the Book

The book is organized in eight chapters that present the results of the comparative evaluation of energy efficiency retrofit programs in the social housing of Canadian cities. The first one introduces research objectives, analytical framework and methodology selected for this research. It uses the housing policy design continuum to identify policy styles and system change/transformation resulting from policy and program implementation. The second chapter provides an overview of national energy efficiency policies affecting the social housing sector and identifies main challenges affecting the implementation of government supported programs targeting energy efficiency retrofits and quality improvements. The third chapter presents highlights from the implementation of CEAP programs in British Columbia with illustration of key program achievements in five case studies. The fourth chapter follows the same approach reviewing key metrics of success in program implementation, focusing on the experience of Toronto, the largest social housing provider in Ontario. Three case studies profile the way public, non-profit and cooperative providers implemented CEAP funding and the results achieved. Similar logic defines the analysis in Chap. 5 focused on Alberta, featuring six case studies in Calgary and Edmonton to illustrate the diversity of challenges and opportunities.

[1]For example, the responses could range from simple building envelope insulation and, installation of energy efficient heating and cooling systems, to solar power and zero net energy developments.

The new wave of energy efficiency retrofit programs is reviewed in the following chapters. Chapter 6 evaluates current practices on energy retrofits in social and affordable housing in British Columbia and Ontario, launched in 2014, highlighting differences and similarities in multiple jurisdictions. The results of program implementation in cities illustrate a shift to more comprehensive retrofits and partnerships capitalizing on the first wave of program funding. Five case studies from Toronto and Vancouver illustrate the environmental, economic and social benefits of more comprehensive retrofits compared in chapter seven. Project details such as costs, reduction of energy consumption and GHG emissions as well as simple return on investment are profiled in the Annex. The final chapter highlights main findings in comparative perspective and provides a broad-based critical reflection on effectiveness and efficiency of federal and provincial programs targeting quality improvements and energy efficiency retrofits in the social housing sector across Canada. It synthesizes this knowledge into a roadmap for future program design and implementation to achieve more strategic change. The process so far can be characterised as 'muddling though' with some positive evolutionary transformation in the social and affordable housing sector. A new '3i' framework is proposed as a conceptual tool to enhance policy design of energy retrofit policies and strategies.

References

Bardhan, A., Edelstein, R. H., & Kroll, C. A. (Eds.). (2012). *Global Housing markets: Crises, policies, and institutions*. NJ: Willey.

Beerepoot, M. (2007). *Energy policy instruments and technical change in the residential building sector*. Amsterdam: IOS Press.

Brandsen, T., van de Donk, W., & Putters, K. (2005). Griffins or chameleons? Hybridity as a permanent and inevitable characteristic of the third sector. *Int J Public Admin, 28*(9/10), 749–765.

Centrum für Energietechnologie. (2008). *Guideline on social housing energy retrofitting financing schemes in EU new member states*. Brussels: Intelligent Energy Europe. https://ec.europa.eu/energy/intelligent/projects.

Cohen, M., March, G., & Olsen, J. (1972). A garbage can model of organizational choice. *Admin Sci Q, 17*(1), 1–25.

Engelund, K., & Wittchen, K. (2008). *European national strategies to move towards very low energy buildings*. Hørsholm: Aalborg University, Danish Building Research Institute.

Forrester, J. (1984). Bounded rationality and the politics of muddling through. *Public Admin Rev, 44*(1), 26–38.

Fuller, M. (2009). *Enabling investments in energy efficiency; a study of energy efficiency programs that reduce first-cost barriers in the residential sector*. Berkeley: University of California, California Institute for Energy and Environment.

Gruis, V., & Nieboer, N. (Eds.). (2004). *Asset management in the social rented sector. Policy and practice in Europe and Australia*. Dortmuth: Springer.

Gruis, V., Tsenkova, S., & Nieboer, N. (Eds.). (2009). *Management of privatised housing: International perspectives*. Chichester: Wiley-Blackwell.

Hamilton, B. (2010). *A comparison of energy efficiency programmes for existing homes in eleven Countries*. Burlington: Vermont Energy Investment Corporation.

Housing Europe. (2019). *The financing of renovation in the social housing sector: A comparative study in 6 European countries*. Brussels: Housing Europe Office.

Itard, L., & Klunder, G. (2007). Comparing environmental impacts of renovated housing stock with new construction. *Building Res Information, 35*(3), 252–267.

Jenkins, D. P. (2010). The value of retrofitting carbon-saving measures into fuel poor social housing. *Energy Policy, 38*(2), 832–839. https://doi.org/10.1016/j.enpol.2009.10.030.

Kickert, W., Klijn, E., & Koppenjan, J. (Eds.). (1997). *Managing complex networks; strategies for the public sector*. London: Sage Publications.

Lindblom, C. (1977). *Politics and markets*. New York: Basic Books.

Lindbloom, C. (1979). Still muddling through. *Public Admin Rev, 39*(6), 517–525.

Linder, S., & Peters, B. (1989). Instruments of government: Perceptions and contexts. *J Public Policy, 9*(1), 35–58.

Lowndes, V., & Skelcher, C. (2002). The dynamics of multi-organizational partnerships: An analysis of changing modes of Governance. *Public Administration, 6*(2), 313–333. https://doi.org/10.1111/1467-9299.00103.

McKinsey & Company. (2009). *Unlocking energy efficiency in the US economy*. Zurich: McKinsey. https://www.sallan.org/pdf-docs/MCKINSEY_US_energy_efficiency.pdf.

Milin, C., & Bullier, A. (2011). *Energy retrofitting of social housing through energy performance contracts a feedback from the FRESH project: France, Italy, United Kingdom*. Brussels: Intelligent Energy Europe (IEE) of the European Commission.

Mlecnik, E., Visscher, H., & van Hal, A. (2010). Barriers and opportunities for labels for highly energy-efficient houses. *Energy Policy, 38*(8), 4592–4603.

Morrison, N. (2013). Meeting the decent homes standard: London housing associations' asset management strategies. *Urban Studies, 50*(12), 2569. { 2587.

Natural Resources Canada. (2006). *The state of energy efficiency in Canada*. Ottawa: Natural Resources Canada.

Niebor, N., Tsenkova, S., Gruis, V., & van Hal, A. (2012). *Energy efficiency in housing management. Policies and practice in eleven countries*. Milton Park: Routledge.

Office of Energy Efficiency. (2009). *Energy efficiency trends in Canada 1990–2007*. Ottawa: Natural Resources Canada.

Peuportier, B., Neumann, U., Dalenback, J.-O., Nesje, A., Csoknyai, T., & Boonstra, C. (2007). Training for renovated energy efficient social housing. CESB 2007 PRAGUE International Conference - Central Europe Towards Sustainable Building, 1.

Pitt, M. (2007). *Linking social housing and energy efficiency*. Ottawa, ON: Social Housing Services Corporation.

Rowlands, I. H., & Stephen, G. (2016). Vulnerable Households and the Smart Grid in Ontario.

Schüle, R. (2009). *Energy efficiency watch; final report on the evaluation of National Energy Efficiency Action Plans*. Berlin: Wuppertal Institute.

Thibert, J. (2007). *Inclusion and social housing practice in Canadian cities: Following the path from good intentions to sustainable projects*. Ottawa: Social Housing Services Corporation.

Toronto and Region Conservation Authority. (2017). *Review of effectiveness of Investments in Renewable Energy for social and affordable housing*. Toronto: Evergreen.

Tsenkova, S. (2003). Housing policy matters: The reform path in central and Eastern Europe: Policy convergence? In S. Tsenkova & S. Lowe (Eds.), *Housing change in central and Eastern Europe* (pp. 193–205). Aldershot: Ashgate Publishing Limited.

Tsenkova, S. (2006). *Ex-post evaluation of social housing programs in Finland*. Paris: Council of Europe Bank.

Tsenkova, S. (2009). *Housing reforms in post-socialist Europe. Lost in transition*. Heidelberg: Springer.

Tsenkova, S. (2013). *Retrofits for the future: Affordable housing and energy efficiency programs in Canada*. Calgary: University of Calgary. Retrieved February 10, 2019, from https://ucalgary.ca/cities/files/cities/EnergyRetrofitsTsenkova2013.pdf.

Tsenkova, S. (2018). Transformative change: Energy-efficiency and social housing retrofits in Canadian cities. *Urban Res Practice, 11*(3), 263–274.

Van Bortel, G., & Elsinga, M. (2007). A network perspective on the Organization of Social Housing in the Netherlands: The case of urban renewal in the Hague. *Housing, Theory and Society, 24*(1), 32–48.

Van Bortel, G., & Mullins, D. (2009). Critical perspectives on network governance in urban regeneration, community involvement and integration. *Journal of Housing and the Built Environment, 24*(2), 203–219.

Van Bortel, G., Gruis, V., Nieuwenhuijzen, J., & Pluijmers, B. (Eds.). (2019). *Affordable housing governance and finance: Innovations, partnerships and comparative perspectives*. Oxon: Routledge.

Weber, L. (1997). Some reflections on barriers to the efficient use of energy. *Energy Policy, 25*(10), 833. {835.

Chapter 2
The Design of Energy Efficiency Programs in Canada: A Social Housing Lens

2.1 The Energy Housing Nexus

The energy efficiency retrofit programs in urban Canada need to be interpreted in the context of increasing commitments to sustainability and environmental protection. This chapter identifies the connection between national and provincial energy policies and efforts to adapt existing housing so that it becomes less energy intensive and more resilient. The nexus concept is the interconnection between the resources energy, water, climate and housing, which cuts across several policy areas. The circular economy increasingly considers the nexus of energy and built environment to identify synergies and trade-offs of policy intervention, so energy efficiency retrofits in housing serve complimentary environmental, social and economic policy objectives (Arman et al. 2009; HUD 2011). Canada is a federal state, governed by ten provinces and three territories, so the policy implementation process is decentralised. Because Canadian provinces have jurisdiction over energy matters within their borders, the federal government works with provincial governments to build consensus on the goals and instruments of energy policies to advance national energy goals (Canadian Energy Efficiency Alliance 2009). This is further complicated due to the country's vast size, where large distances between production and consumption as well as diverse climatic regions influence specific provincial energy efficiency targets and policies.

At the national level, as a signatory of the *United Nations Framework Convention on Climate Change*, Canada has set the target of lowering 30% of Canada's GHG emissions compared to the 2005 level by 2030 (Government of Canada 2018a). In 2016, Canada produced 704 megatonnes of carbon dioxide equivalent, out of which 81.4 megatonnes were from the building sector (approximately 12%) (Government of Canada 2018b). Regulatory efforts include the enforcement of *Energy Efficiency Act 2012* to mandate the use of energy-efficient products in construction and a new *National Energy Building Code* 2017 to raise the technical standards and requirements for energy-efficient design (National Resources Canada 2019).

S. Tsenkova, *Energy Efficient Affordable Housing*,
https://doi.org/10.1007/978-3-030-69563-7_2

Energy savings in the built environment are a priority on the political agenda due to their potential to improve the security of energy supply, reduce greenhouse gas (GHG) emissions and respond to climate change imperatives (Engelund and Wittchen 2008; Itard and Klunder 2007). The housing sector accounts for 17% of secondary energy use and for 16% of GHG emissions with over 80% of the residential energy use related to space and hot water heating (Natural Resources Canada 2006). While experimental technologies in new housing and Leadership in Energy Efficient Design (LEED) certified buildings have demonstrated a potential 40% reduction in energy consumption, the impact remains limited due to the pilot nature of these projects (CMHC 2008). Natural Resources Canada (NRCan) is the lead federal agency administering the *Energy Efficiency Act* and managing the *ecoEnergy for Efficiency Initiative*. Federal efforts center on regulatory and fiscal instruments. The diversity and the autonomy at the provincial level are both a challenge and an opportunity, leading to a lack of harmonization of policies across provinces and territories (IEA 2010).

To meet *Canada's Paris Agreement* commitments for GHG reduction, the *Low Carbon Economy Leadership Fund* was set up in 2017 by the government of Canada to provide capital support over a 5-year period to increase energy efficiency in buildings and to reduce GHG emissions (Government of Canada 2018b). The $1.4 billion is allocated according to the population of the provinces and territories (Government of Canada 2018b). Provincial governments partner with federal agencies to implement these initiatives. EfficiencyBC is a jointly funded program by the federal and provincial government with each contributing $12 million under the *Low Carbon Economy Leadership Fund* to achieve the province's reduction in GHG emission (Province of British Columbia 2018). Under *Ontario's Climate Change Action Plan* released in 2015, strategies to reduce GHG emissions to 80% below 1990 levels by 2050, are supported through the *Green Ontario Fund* (GreenON). In addition, a variety of housing retrofit programs were supported across the province introducing the latest low-carbon and carbon-free energy technologies (Housing Services Corporation 2018).

The federal government established a regulatory framework for energy efficiency through the *EnerGuide Home Rating System* and regulations under the *Energy Efficiency Act*. However, provincial governments have autonomy in decision-making affecting the housing sector, which has resulted in a wide variety of financial programs and standards for energy efficiency. Energy efficiency in housing is promoted at several levels: (1) the level of appliances used within the building; (2) the level of site planning and building envelope; and (3) the level of land uses to deliver more compact and complete communities. Policies first targeted appliances and heating and cooling systems in housing through the *EnerGuide* rating system (mandatory since 1995) and *Energy Star* rated appliances (introduced in 2001), then shifted to regulations for new home construction (R-2000) and LEED certification (Tsenkova and Youssef 2012). In the last decade federal and provincial programs targeted energy efficiency retrofits in existing housing, combining regulatory and financial instruments. Given the fact that 58% of the residential buildings across Canada are single detached dwellings, small scale programs provided homeowners with incentives to replace heating and ventilation systems with energy efficient furnaces as well as carry out window replacement and weatherization measures. Overall, the implementation of housing energy efficiency measures had a slow start due to a decentralized policy-making framework (Canadian Energy Efficiency Alliance 2009).

NRCan uses financial incentives to encourage end-users to adopt energy efficiency and renewable energy technologies and practices. The $60 million *ecoENERGY for Buildings and Houses,* introduced in 2007, encourages the construction and retrofit of energy-efficient homes. The *Energy Efficiency Act* (2009), gives the Government of Canada the authority to enforce regulations regarding performance and labelling requirements for energy-using products, including doors and windows (CMHC 2009; Canadian Home Builders' Association 2011). The province of Ontario was the first jurisdiction in Canada to mandate *EnerGuide 80* levels. This means that homes built after 2011 will have a 35% increase in energy efficiency compared to homes built before 2006. Ontario's *2006 Building Code* requires energy-efficient standards to be implemented for residential and institutional buildings. In BC, a 'green' *Building Code* that specifies requirements for energy and water efficiency for all buildings came into effect in 2008. Amendments to *BC's Energy Efficiency Act*, adopted in 2009, raised the energy performance of residential buildings.

Municipalities also play an important role in energy efficiency through the Federation of Canadian Municipalities (FCM), which manages the $550 million *Green Municipal Fund* and the Partners for Climate Protection network. Municipalities design and implement a variety of energy efficiency programs. In addition to governments, utility companies play a significant role in the implementation of programs promoting energy efficiency. Most electricity and natural gas distributors/retailers have established demand management and energy efficiency programs (e.g. thermostats, furnace and water heater replacement programs, PowerSmart, PowerWise, PowerSense, etc.). Demand side management programs typically include information and education initiatives, low-interest loans or subsidies for the installation of energy-efficient technologies, direct or free installation of energy-efficient technologies, performance contracting, and market transformation initiatives.

2.2 Energy Efficiency Programs in the Social Housing Sector

2.2.1 Canada Economic Action Plan Energy Retrofit Programs

The first systematic energy efficiency retrofit programs affecting social housing in Canada were launched in 2009. *The Renewable Energy Initiative* was launched in 2009 with $70 million in funding for energy efficiency upgrades in existing social

Table 2.1 Canada's economic action plan renovation and retrofit of existing social housing

Provincially/Territorially administered[a]		
Province/Territory	Funds allocated (Federal $M)[b]	Projects[c]
Newfoundland and Labrador	$21.26	283
Prince Edward Island	$2.22	40
Nova Scotia	$34.34	604
New Brunswick	$26.34	438
Quebec	$155.54	1519
Ontario	$352.16	5817
Manitoba	$61.70	336
Saskatchewan	$51.08	831
Alberta	$45.38	1105
British Columbia	$88.82	105
Northwest Territories	$4.68	28
Yukon	$0.86	19
Nunavut	$5.62	230
Total	$850.00	11,355

Source: Based on program data CMHC (2012)
[a]Program details available at http://cmhc.ca/en/inpr/afhoce/fias/fias_017.cfm
[b]All funding for 2009–10 and 2010–11 (fiscal) has been allocated
[c]Total numbers of projects underway or completed as at December 31, 2011

housing projects and new affordable housing projects. The federal and provincial governments contributed equally to this investment. *Canada's Economic Action Plan* provided $850 million over 2 years for the renovation and retrofit of existing social housing, plus a further $475 million to build new rental housing for low-income seniors and persons with disabilities. These new housing investments addressed Canada's climate change and environmental goals. The *Economic Action Plan* included $2 billion for new and existing social housing, plus $2 billion in loans to municipalities for housing-related infrastructure. Federal funding allocation to different provinces with a corresponding number of projects supported is presented in Table 2.1.

This joint federal and provincial program led to improved energy efficiency, and supported the installation of renewable energy systems in existing and new affordable housing (Office of Energy Efficiency 2009). The federal funding was matched by provincial investment on a 50/50 cost-sharing basis. For example, the province of Ontario channeled $704 million into repair and energy efficiency retrofits of social housing. In British Columbia a total of $164 million was allocated to housing projects in the BC Housing portfolio to develop, manage and operating environmentally sustainable affordable housing. The implementation of *'Livegreen: A Housing Sustainability Action Plan'* included the retrofitting of more than 7500 directly managed social housing projects to increase energy efficiency and environmental performance. Another initiative, *Solar BC*, was funded by the Ministry of Energy, Mines and Petroleum Resources and delivered in cooperation with Natural Resources Canada *ecoENERGY for Renewable Heat* program. It provided support to affordable housing owners and not-for-profit social housing societies for the installation of a solar water system. Provincial utilities offered additional opportunities for investing in energy efficiency and reducing energy costs. In Alberta, federal funding was matched by the province and directly allocated to over 120 housing management bodies for quality, safety and energy retrofit improvements. The evaluation of program implementation is provided in Chaps. 3, 4 and 5 in this book.

In addition to these funds, CMHC administered a system of grants to social housing providers managing social housing under CMHC agreements. The territorial distribution of these funds—a total of $150 million—is presented in Table 2.2.

2.2.2 A New Wave of Energy Retrofit Programs

The first *National Housing Strategy "Place to Call Home"* launched in 2017 is an important accelerator of previous policy initiatives. It commits $55 billion over 10 years premised on partnerships, people and communities. The Strategy offers a vision of inclusive community renewal on a national scale. The targets are ambitious:

- 385,000 community housing units protected and another 50,000 units created in the community housing sector;
- 300,000 housing units renewed representing three times the units renewed under 2005–2015 federal programs;
- 100,000 new housing units built representing four times the units built under 2005–2015 federal programs (Government of Canada 2017).

The *National Housing Co-Investment Fund* addresses one of the priorities by providing long term, low-interest loans for the construction and revitalization of affordable housing. The focus of this fund is to develop energy efficient, accessible and socially inclusive housing. The implementation process has been limited, particularly as far as investment in existing social housing is concerned.

The implementation of these new housing policy commitments capitalizes on results achieved through the CEAP retrofit programs. A variety of provincial initiatives were implemented with varied degree of success—these are reviewed in detail in chapters six and seven in this book. In Ontario, policies and programs to retrofit affordable housing for energy efficiency respond to the efforts to combat climate change and to improve the affordable housing stock. The *Green Ontario Fund Social Housing Program* (GreenON) and the *Social Housing Apartment Improvement Program* (SHAIP) committed $92 million to reduce GHG emissions in social housing developments through the *Social Housing Apartment Retrofit Program* (SHARP) targeting high-rise social housing and the *Social Housing Electricity Efficiency Program* (SHEEP) geared towards electrically heated houses and townhouses. The GreenON promised to invest $25 million in retrofits of social housing apartment buildings across the province introducing the latest low-carbon and carbon-free energy technologies (Housing Services Corporation 2018). Lastly,

Table 2.2 Renovation and retrofit of social housing—CMHC administered

Province/ Territory[a]	Cooperative housing		Non-profit housing		Urban native housing		Total	
	Funds allocated (Federal $M)[b]	Projects[c]	Funds allocated (Federal $M)[b]	Projects[c]	Funds allocated (Federal $M)[b]	Projects[c]	Funds allocated (Federal $M)[b]	Projects[c]
Prince Edward Island	$0.50	9	$1.50	40	$0.20	9	$2.20	58
Quebec	$33.20	509	$19.20	170	$0.10	3	$52.50	682
Ontario	$40.20	259	n/a	n/a	$0.30	40	$40.50	299
Manitoba	n/a	n/a	n/a	n/a	$0.30	12	$0.30	12
Alberta	$3.60	33	$7.30	80	$0.30	9	$11.20	122
British Columbia	$43.20	138	n/a	n/a	n/a	n/a	$43.20	138
Yukon	n/a	n/a	n/a	n/a	$0.10	1	$0.10	1
Total	$120.70	948	$28.00	290	$1.30	74	$150.00	1312

[a]Applies only to provinces and territories where CMHC continues to directly administer existing federally-assisted social housing projects
[b]All funding for 2009–10 and 2010–11 (fiscal) has been fully taken up
[c]Total number of projects underway or completed as at December 31, 2011

the SHAIP promised $556 million for social housing high-rise apartment buildings over 4 years across Ontario, contingent on the revenue received from the cap-and-trade program (Government of Ontario 2018). These programs, despite their good start, however, had a more limited scope due to changes in provincial government priorities and cancellation of funding commitments.

Energy efficiency retrofit programs in British Columbia, such as the *Social Housing Retrofit Support Program*, the *EfficiencyBC Social Housing Incentive Program* as well as the *Capital Renewal Fund* aim at GHG reductions. Energy retrofits in social housing in Vancouver are often joint efforts administered by BC Housing with support from the BC Non-profit Housing Association and the main energy service companies. In Alberta, energy efficiency retrofit policies were an integral part of *Alberta's Affordable Housing Strategy*. It aimed at maintaining and improving the conditions of existing affordable housing stock (Government of Alberta 2017). Implementation was initiated with the launch of the *Affordable Housing Energy Savings Program* (AHESP) with a budget of $25 million to increase the environmental and financial sustainability of publicly owned affordable housing, which was discontinued due to changes in the provincial government (Government of Alberta 2018).

2.3 The Social Housing Sector in Canada

Social housing in Canada is less than 6% of the housing stock (630,000 units). The sector operates in a market-driven environment for the provision, allocation and maintenance of housing, with limited government support. Subsidized housing includes rent-geared-to-income (RGI), social housing, public housing, government-assisted housing, non-profit housing, and cooperative housing. The social housing sector is operated by public, non-profit organizations, cooperatives or intentional communities. It may or may not receive operating subsidies from different levels of government. About 49% of the social housing is publicly owned by provinces/territories and municipalities, 40% non-profit and cooperative housing for mixed-income tenants, 10% is not-profit and cooperative housing for low income tenants and 1% is owned by CMHC. Most of the affordable and social housing targets low-income tenants (see Fig. 2.1). It is difficult to capture this diversity as it has evolved over the last 70 years, but the terms 'social' and 'affordable' housing are used interchangeably. Recent housing policies have started to redefine 'social housing' in relationship to public and provincially owned stock, while the term 'affordable housing' is related to mixed income developments owned by not-for-profit and cooperative providers.

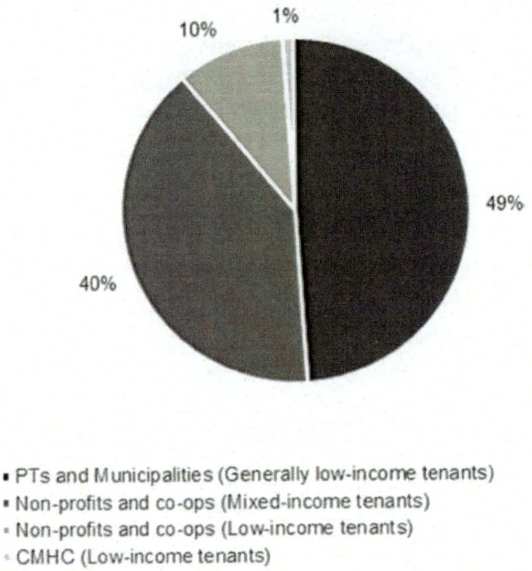

Fig. 2.1 Ownership of Social Housing in Canada. Source: Interview data, CMHC Policy Division manager, 2019

2.3.1 Path Dependency

Social and affordable housing in Canada is path dependent and reflects the evolution of housing policy. It is funded through agreements between the federal and provincial governments (and territories), and between these two levels of governments and social housing providers. These agreements set out the parameters of different housing programs, rent setting strategies and eligibility criteria. The start of substantial government involvement in social housing dates back to the post-war years when homes were built for veterans (see Fig. 2.2). CMHC's limited dividend rental housing program encouraged private developers to provide purpose built rental housing through low-cost, long-term mortgages, limiting profits to 5%. In 1949 joint federal-provincial programs were launched to construct publicly owned housing for low-income families, persons with disabilities, and seniors. The programs operated till 1985 resulting in 205,000 dwelling units, thus creating an important legacy in Canadian housing policy. Criticisms of large scale public housing projects led to the introduction of mixed income non-profit housing programs since 1973. Under the program, loans were made directly by CMHC for up to 100% of the capital cost to housing providers building 236,000 social housing units between 1973 and 1993 (CMHC 2014).

The 1990s marked a radical departure from these models with a devolution of federal housing responsibilities to the provinces and territories and the elimination of

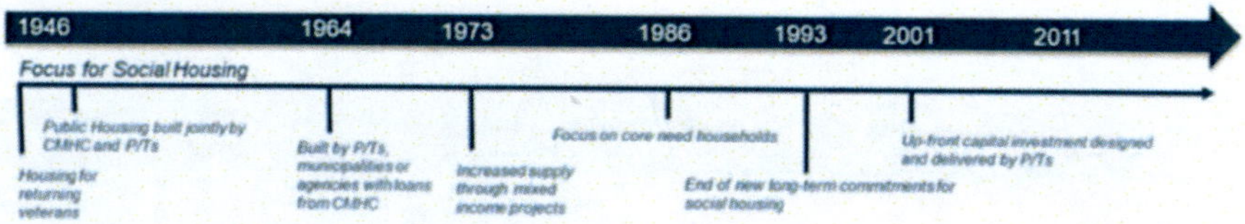

Fig. 2.2 Milestones in Canadian Housing Policy. Source: Author

federally funded programs. While social housing is a provincial responsibility, the federal government supported the sector through a variety of financial instruments and programs that were largely discontinued in 1993. The devolution started in the mid-1980s with provinces gradually moving away from the sector and eventually 'passing the buck' to municipalities and community partnerships. By the end of the 1990s a housing crisis emerged due to housing shortages in large cities and increasing homelessness, coupled with a supply shortage of social housing and long waiting lists. This prompted a reengagement by the federal government in 2001 through the *Affordable Housing Initiative (AHI),* a multilateral agreement between federal, provincial and municipal governments. This initiative consisted of two phases cost shared on a 50/50 basis (CMHC 2010a, b). The first phase, with a budget of $680 million, was to create new rental housing and to renovate existing social housing, while the second phase, with a budget of $320 million, was to create housing for low-income households, aboriginals, people with disabilities, recent immigrants and seniors (Leone and Carroll 2010). Overall, the funding resulted in 4000–6000 social housing units per year, a fraction of the approximately 20,000 social housing units that were funded annually from the mid-1960s to the mid-1990s (Hulchanski 2020). Today, 1.7 million households in Canada are in core housing need with over 80% of those being renters (CMHC n.d.)

2.3.2 *The Housing Continuum*

The Housing Continuum is a helpful way of understanding the spectrum of affordable housing options and the laddering of housing experiences of people in the housing market (Fig. 2.3).

At one end are the emergency shelters and short-term opportunities in transitional housing to alleviate a housing crisis. Long-term supportive housing is for people with special needs, health issues, disabilities, seniors in need of supportive care. These units operate with subsidized rent of 30% of tenants' pre-tax income. Subsidized housing includes rent-geared-to-income (RGI), social housing, public housing, government-assisted housing, and community not-for-profit housing. It provides supportive living to low-income tenants. At the other end of the housing continuum is near market affordable housing operated by not-for-profit and cooperative providers with rent levels set at 10% below area-based median market rents. Affordable

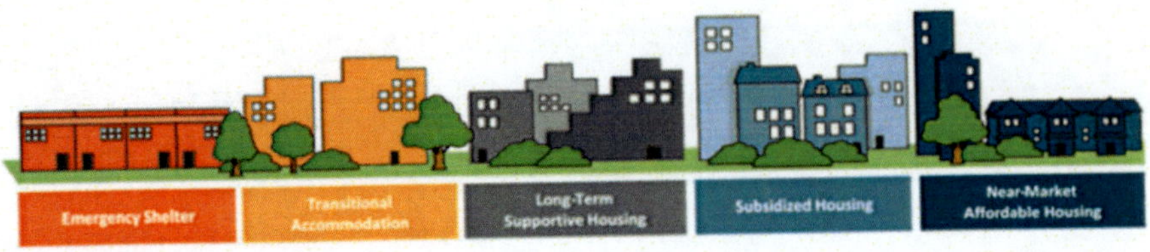

Fig. 2.3 The affordable housing continuum. Source: Adapted from Ministry of Housing and Seniors, Government of Alberta (2020)

homeownership for key workers, supported through equity loans and shared capital appreciation also falls in this category. The level of government support declines in this part of the affordable housing continuum, although there are a number of supply—and demand-side subsidies that operate with various degree of intensity and targeting across the spectrum of affordable and social housing. In addition to bricks-and-mortar affordable housing, rent supplement programs support financially the cost of housing for low-income households by reducing their shelter-to-income-ratio (Tsenkova 2013).

Public housing accounts for 2% of Canada's housing stock and is owned by local and provincial government authorities. It is managed by public non-profit organizations and housing companies established by municipalities. The Board of Directors is appointed by a municipal council and is composed of council members and tenants. Some of the largest public housing landlords are in Toronto and Vancouver. *Private non-profit organizations* range from ethnic or religious groups to special purpose organizations that accommodate seniors people with disabilities, and more broadly, low-income households. Some of the non-profit providers build one project for the group, but in larger cities community-based organizations build several projects (Dreier and Hulchanski 1993). The sector is very diverse and dependent on government funding and philanthropy both in terms of supply and demand-side support. *The cooperative sector* consists of 2200 housing cooperatives, each containing on average 50 to 80 units; more than 40% of the tenants receive a federal or provincial housing allowance, while the rest pay market rents. Direct involvement of resident members in committees or elected Board of Directors is a key feature of cooperative governance (Dreier and Hulchanski 1993).

Eligibility criteria for social housing vary according to the funding regime under which it was developed. Public housing developed between 1974 and 1986 needs to be allocated to households with low incomes, while social and affordable housing developed since 1986 is targeted to households that meet 'core housing need' requirements defined by a measure of suitability (overcrowding), adequateness (need for repairs) and affordability (over 30% of gross income) in addition to an income threshold test (Ditch et al. 2001). Social rents are set as a share of tenants' income rather than being property-based. Rents for social housing range from 25% to 30% of household income and increase to 'net cost' or 'low end of the market' for higher income households (Steele 2007).

The majority of social housing stock is over 40 years old and is in need of repairs and modernization. Operating costs in public and non-profit housing are on average higher than the operating costs of co-ops. Public housing tends to be older with higher turnover, which contributes to higher operation costs. The allocation predominantly to low income households also places additional requirements for ongoing social service support and capital to bridge the revenue/expenditure gap. Most co-ops and non-profit providers, have inadequate capital reserves and are not in a financial position to fulfill upkeep, major maintenance costs or essential capital replacements (Pearson 2010).

2.4 Concluding Comments

While newly launched federal initiatives through the *National Housing Strategy* and climate change energy programs provide a few years of funding to address some long-standing problems in the social housing sector, large scale energy efficient retrofits needed require systematic support through well integrated regulatory, fiscal and financial measures. The lack of a long-term strategy for social and affordable housing in Canada is a challenge and within this context provincial initiatives may have limited results. Some estimates suggest that at least 18,000 to 20,000 new social housing units need to be built every year, plus 7000 repaired and renovated, to adequately address a growing need for affordable rental housing across Canada (see Wellesley Institute 2010). Many social housing providers used CEAP funds to renovate and retrofit social housing, but the program was terminated and the new wave of provincial programs in energy efficiency retrofits driven by climate change commitments were short-lived (Government of Canada 2016).

Since the federal downloading of responsibility for social housing, the provinces have become completely autonomous in managing and administrating their social housing stock. All federal controls have been removed and provinces are free to allocate funding for developing social housing as they see fit. Provinces are also free to reduce the size of their portfolio by disposing of aging stock, which includes the stock previously under provincial-federal partnership. The autonomy gained by the provinces includes their ability to modify and rationalize the housing programs inherited from the federal government. The downside of expanded provincial government social housing responsibilities is constrained investment in the maintenance and rehabilitation of the aging stock owned by public and non-profit housing providers. Although co-ops and other non-profit housing providers are responsible for meeting their upgrading and maintenance costs, provinces are indirectly involved by subsidizing the cost of those projects and paying the rent-geared-to-income (RGI) assistance.

The allocation predominantly to low income households also places additional requirements for ongoing social service support and capital to bridge the revenue/expenditure gap. Co-ops and non-profit community groups are also limited in their potential to intensify renovation efforts due to their small size and limited institutional capacity to develop portfolio management strategies. These changes define the context for evaluation of different energy retrofit programs in Canadian cities presented in the following chapters.

References

Arman, M., Zuo, J., Wilson, L., Zillante, G., & Pullen, S. (2009). Challenges of responding to sustainability with implications for affordable housing. *Ecological Economics, 68*, 3034–3041.

Canada Mortgage and Housing Corporation (CMHC). (2008). *Analysis of renewable energy potential in the residential sector. Technical series*. Ottawa: CMHC.

Canada Mortgage and Housing Corporation (CMHC). (2009). *Renovation and retrofit of existing social housing: Provincially/territorially administered renovation and retrofit of existing social housing initiative.* Retrieved November 30 from http://www.cmhc.ca/housingactionplan/reresoho/lipr.cfm

Canadian Energy Efficiency Alliance. (2009). *National energy efficiency report card*. Ottawa: Canadian Energy Efficiency Alliance.

Canadian Home Builders' Association. (2011). *Energy use and greenhouse gas emission performance in Canadian homes since 1990: 1990–2008 update*. Ottawa: Canadian Home Builders' Association.

CMHC. (2010a). *Application guidelines: Renovation and retrofit of existing social housing administered by CMHC.* Retrieved November 30 from http://www.cmhc.ca/housingactionplan/reresoho/index.cfm

CMHC. (2010b). *CHS - public funds and National Housing Act (Social Housing) 2009*. Ottawa: Canada Mortgage and Housing Corporation.

CMHC. (2012). *CEAP- renovation and retrofit projects*. Ottawa: Canada Mortgage and Housing Corporation. Retrieved November 12, 2012 from http://www.cmhc.ca/housingactionplan/reresoho/lipr.cfm.

CMHC. (2014). *The Canadian housing observer*. Ottawa: CMHC.

CMHC. (n.d.). *Core Housing Need (Census-based and NHS-based housing indicators and data)*. Retrieved from https://www03.cmhc-schl.gc.ca/hmip-pimh/en/TableMapChart/CoreHousingNeedMethodology

Ditch, J., Lewis, A., & Wilcox, S. (2001). *Social housing, tenure and housing allowance: An international review*. New York: Department of Works and Pensions.

Dreier, P., & Hulchanski, J. D. (1993). The role of nonprofit housing in Canada and the United States: Some comparisons. *Housing Policy Debate, 4*, 43–80.

Engelund, K., & Wittchen, K. (2008). *European national strategies to move towards very low energy buildings*. Hørsholm: Aalborg University, Danish Building Research Institute.

Government of Alberta. (2017). *Alberta's provincial affordable housing strategy summary*. Edmonton: Ministry of Seniors and Housing. Retrieved from https://open.alberta.ca/dataset/18c109bc-e567-4f61-b9e4-8973b0b246c4/resource/66dafa3a-c307-441a-8dd8-5c7aac66d025/download/pahssummary.pdf.

Government of Alberta. (2018). *Program guide to affordable housing energy savings program*. Edmonton: Ministry of Seniors and Housing.

Government of Alberta. (2020). *Affordable Housing Review Panel*. Edmonton: Ministry of Seniors and Housing, July.

Government of Canada. (2016). *Energy efficiency regulations*. Retrieved from https://www.canada.ca/en/natural-resources-canada/news/2016/04/energy-efficiency-regulations.html

Government of Canada. (2017). *Canada's national housing strategy*. Retrieved from https://www.placetocallhome.ca/pdfs/Canada-National-Housing-Strategy.pdf

Government of Canada. (2018a). *Canadian environmental - sustainability indicators greenhouse gas emissions.* Gatineau: Ministry of Environment and Climate Change. Retrieved March 19, 2019, from https://www.canada.ca/content/dam/eccc/documents/pdf/cesindicators/greenhouse-gas-emissions/greenhouse-gas-emissions-en.pdf.

Government of Canada. (2018b). *Low carbon economy fund: allocations to provinces and territories under the low carbon economy leadership fund.* Retrieved from Government of Canada: https://www.canada.ca/en/environment-climate-change/news/2017/06/low_carbon_economyfundallocationstoprovincesandterritoriesundert.html

Government of Ontario. (2018). *Investment in affordable housing*. Retrieved March 3, 2019, from Ministry of Municipal affairs and housing: http://www.mah.gov.on.ca/Page17675.aspx

Housing Services Corporation. (2018). *GreenON Social Housing Program - Program Guidelines.* Retrieved March 1, 2019, from https://www.hscorp.ca/wp-content/uploads/2018/02/One-Pager-GreenON-Final.pdf

Hulchanski, D. J. (2020). Private rental housing in Canada's four largest metropolitan areas: Trends and prospects. In S. Tsenkova (Ed.), *The future of affordable housing*. Calgary: University of Calgary, SAPL.

International Energy Agency (IEA). (2010). *Energy policies of IEA countries - Canada 2009 Review*. Paris: International Energy Agency.

Itard, L., & Klunder, G. (2007). Comparing environmental impacts of renovated housing stock with new construction. *Building Research & Information, 35*(3), 252–267.

Leone, R., & Carroll, B. W. (2010). Decentralisation and devolution in Canadian SOCIAL housing policy. *Environment and Planning C: Government and Policy, 28*, 389–404.

National Resources Canada. (2019). *National Energy Code of Canada for Buildings 2017.* Retrieved from https://nrc.canada.ca/en/certifications-evaluations-standards/codes-canada/codes-canada-publications/national-energy-code-canada-buildings-2017

Natural Resources Canada. (2006). *The state of energy efficiency in Canada*. Ottawa: Natural Resources Canada.

Office of Energy Efficiency. (2009). *Energy efficiency trends in Canada 1990–2007*. Ottawa: Natural Resources Canada.

Pearson, S. N. (2010). *Financing capital improvements and renovation of soical housing in Ontario*. Ontario: Social Housing Services Corporation.

Province of British Columbia. (2018). *CleanBC.* Retrieved March 23, 2019, from https://blog.gov.bc.ca/app/uploads/sites/436/2019/02/CleanBC_Full_Report_Updated_Mar2019.pdf

Steele, M. (2007). Canadian housing allowances. In P. A. Kemp (Ed.), *Housing allowances in comparative perspective*. Bristol: The Policy Press, University of Bristol.

Tsenkova, S. (2013). *Retrofits for the future: Affordable housing and energy efficiency programs in Canada*. Calgary: University of Calgary. Retrieved February 10, 2019, from https://ucalgary.ca/cities/files/cities/EnergyRetrofitsTsenkova2013.pdf.

Tsenkova, S., & Youssef, K. (2012). Canada. Energy efficiency retrofits: Policy solutions for sustainable social housing. In S. Tsenkova, N. Niebor, V. Gruis, & J. van Hal (Eds.), *Energy efficiency in housing management: Policies and practice in eleven countries*. London: Routledge.

U.S. Department of Housing and Urban Development (HUD). (2011). *Evidence matters: Transforming knowledge into housing and community development policy. Quantifying Energy Efficiency in Multifamily Rental Housing.* Retrieved April 8, 2012 from http://www.huduser.org/portal/periodicals/em/summer11/index.html

Wellesley Institute. (2010). *Precarious housing in Canada*. Toronto: Wellesley Institute Report.

Chapter 3
Beyond Energy Efficiency: Investing in Social and Affordable Housing in Vancouver

3.1 Introduction

This chapter reviews investment programs implemented in British Columbia (BC) and Vancouver through *Canada's Economic Action Plan 2009–2011 (CEAP)*. Program delivery required co-operation between federal and provincial governments and housing providers. The primary goal of the program was to provide funding for improvements in the quality and energy efficiency of social housing in the province, while contributing to job creation.

The implementation process was examined in the context of limited government support for social housing in Canada. The sector is small, less than 6% of the housing stock (630,000 dwellings). BC has over 53,000 social housing units, about 9% of the total for Canada.

The chapter focuses on the financial and institutional mechanisms and types of retrofits in the provincial, non-profit and cooperative housing portfolio achieved through CEAP and other provincial programs in BC. The research is exploratory and is the first overview of these policies with an emphasis on challenges and opportunities/achievements. Data from a series of interviews with policy makers and housing portfolio managers suggested that significant improvements have materialised, some focusing on energy efficiency measures, others addressing deferred maintenance and deterioration in the aging stock. The implementation has led to more strategic assessment of capital investment needs, coupled with energy efficiency audits, across the social housing portfolio. Evidence from case studies pointed to a particular emphasis on financing building envelope and technical installation retrofits, not necessarily with the highest return on investment.

Research methodology included a literature review, content analysis of major policy documents and policy briefs, and input from 19 key informant interviews with policy makers, program administrators and portfolio managers using program funds. Information gained through interviews was supplemented by site visits to several projects and an in-depth analysis of three best examples of comprehensive

S. Tsenkova, *Energy Efficient Affordable Housing*,
https://doi.org/10.1007/978-3-030-69563-7_3

renovation and energy efficiency retrofits in Vancouver. The three case studies were selected by senior asset management specialists at BC Housing. The provincial entity manages about half of the social housing in the province and has received most of the CEAP funding. The other two case studies featured retrofits in two Vancouver coops supported through CMHC funding. These projects were selected from an officially published list of cooperative projects based on the relatively large amount of funding and the agreement of the Board to participate in the study.

3.2 Policy Framework for Energy Efficiency Retrofits in the Social Housing Sector

CEAP was launched by the federal government to support energy efficiency retrofits in social housing. It was an integral part of the economic stimulus package and supported other policy initiatives targeting an efficient response to climate change. Its implementation in BC complemented other programs in the province and the partnership mechanisms in the social housing sector that have evolved in the last few years. The 2007 *Energy Plan of British Columbia* combined a variety of policy tools to improve energy use, including codes and standards as well as communicative outreach to stakeholders. New energy efficiency regulations under the *Energy Efficiency Act* and *BC Building Code* set reductions of up to 27% for new homes and 18% for new commercial and institutional buildings, compared to the 1997 *Model National Energy Code for Buildings* (Government of BC 2007, 2009). The *BC Energy Efficient Buildings Strategy* targeted a 33% reduction in GHG emissions from 2007 levels by 2020 as well as electricity self-sufficiency by 2016 (Tsenkova and Youssef 2012). The strategy spurred an investment of $30 million by the BC Ministry of Energy, Mines and Petroleum Resources (MEMPR) for energy efficiency retrofits in the social housing sector through *BC LiveSmart* (Interview data, Ministry official, January 2012).

Since 2009, CEAP funding provided a solid financial framework for renovation and energy efficiency retrofits. Administered through the *Housing Renovation Partnership (HRP)*, $177 million of federal and provincial funds supported repairs and retrofits at 81 social housing developments in BC, with $13 million invested in single room occupancy housing (BC Housing 2010b). Another separate stream of $43 million was administered by CMHC and allocated to non-profit and cooperative social housing providers operating under long-term agreements with CMHC (see Table 3.1).

Table 3.1 Capital program investment in social housing in BC

Program	Funding source	Amount invested	Output
CEAP Renovation and Retrofit of Social Housing	Economic Action Plan/ Housing Renovation Partnership	$164 million	105 housing developments (includes provincial and non-profit housing)
CEAP Renovation and Retrofit of Social Housing for Housing Co-operative	Economic Action Plan/ CMHC	$43 million	138 co-ops
LiveSmart BC: Efficiency Incentive Program	MEMPR	$30 million	26 housing developments

Source: BC Housing (2010a) and CMHC (2009)

3.3 Energy Intensity in BC Social Housing

The social housing sector in BC consists of 53,467 dwellings in seven regions across the province. BC Housing manages half of the social housing in the province. The BC non-profit housing sector includes approximately 600 societies, from regional to city-specific societies. Over 90% of the sector consists of small organizations owning 1 to 5 buildings each, with about 36% of the social housing concentrated in Vancouver. The social housing in Vancouver consists predominantly of apartments (45%), followed by townhouses as the second most popular housing form (City Green Solutions 2010). Small-scale social housing providers also exist, largely as a result of idiosyncratic subsidy arrangements, changing systems of financial support, and specific target groups such as special needs housing (Hulchanski 2004).

The Strategic Energy Management Plan, commissioned by MEMPR in conjunction with the BC Non-Profit Housing Association (BCNPHA), provided an initial evaluation of energy performance and opportunities for intervention in the non-profit housing sector. The study found out that the average energy intensity of most non-profit apartment buildings was higher than the BC average.[1] For example, the average energy intensity for an apartment building in BC was 0.86 GJ/m^2 (239 kWh/m^2) compared to 1.36 GJ/m^2 (377 kWh/m^2) in the non-profit housing sector (City Green Solutions 2010).[2] Apartment buildings also had the highest heating and gas use and the largest percentage of hydroelectricity use in the sector and produced the

[1]There is also higher energy intensity in buildings constructed between 1996 and 2010 (Green City Solutions 2010).

[2]From a sample size of 43 solely operated buildings, 35% have energy intensities above the provincial average. Where providers pay all utility charges, the energy intensity is the highest 2 GJ/m^2 (556 kWh/m^2) (City Green Solutions 2010).

most CO_2 (City Green Solutions 2010). Therefore, apartment buildings provided the largest energy saving opportunity within the social housing sector.[3]

In addition to high energy intensity, much of the social housing stock has structural and technical problems related to backlogs in maintenance, repairs, and lifecycle replacement of roofs, elevators, and heating and cooling installations. The replacement of asbestos, which was widely used in developments from the 1960s and 1970s, as well as mold caused by improper ventilation and/or poor insulation, have made implementing energy efficiency retrofits more demanding. In BC, social housing was built anywhere from 1930 to the early 2000s, and was constructed quickly and with limited budgets in order to address housing shortages (Interview data, Policy Advisor, BC Non-Profit Housing Association, February 2012). Low rents and less in senior government funding have resulted in critical conditions in some properties where high energy intensity is related to outdated building envelopes and technical installations.

In the past decade, a number of advances in energy efficiency technologies and updates to the building code have resulted in improved residential building construction techniques including better quality insulation, ventilation and utility distribution systems (CMHC 2001; Arman et al. 2009).[4] *The Strategic Energy Management Plan* identified reduction of average energy intensity in social housing, particularly in apartment buildings, as a priority. It was estimated that a 16–23% reduction in energy use in the social housing sector can be achieved through energy saving technologies and tenant education (City Green Solutions 2010). Furthermore, it was estimated that each percentage of energy reduction in the non-profit housing sector would result in $500,000 in energy saving annually (City Green Solutions 2010).

3.4 Implementation Framework

An analysis of the implementation framework for three energy efficiency programs in the BC social housing sector revealed differences and similarities. The analysis focused on institutional and financial arrangements and program management. With respect to financial mechanisms, as identified in Table 3.2, all three programs provided grants to eligible social housing providers, one used Energy Service Companies (ESCOs) to administer program implementation, and there were isolated experiments with power purchasing agreements and pay-as-you-save implemented by utility companies.

[3]The intensity is reduced if there is a lower amount of energy consumed (U.S. Department of Energy 2008).

[4]According to the Canadian Home Builders' Association, between 1990 and 2008 GHG emissions in the residential sector in BC rose by 3.5%, which is low compared to Alberta, which grew by 31.9% and Ontario at 17.9% (Canadian Home Builders' Association 2011).

Table 3.2 Financial mechanisms for energy efficiency upgrades

Mechanism	Brief description
Additional Financial Support	Financial support provided by grants, incentives or programs
Energy Service Companies (ESCOs)	Energy savings achieved are used to pay back the cost of the project or to reinvest for capital upgrades
Power Purchasing Agreements	Installation of a solar thermal hot water heater, where billed energy used serves as payment for the system
Pay-As-You-Save	Energy savings achieved through levied meters

Source: Adapted from City Green Solutions (2010), p. 36

Program delivery was managed in two ways: through an intermediary third party or through a self-managed process. BC Housing, which received all $164 million of its funding through the *Housing Renovation Partnership* (HRP), used third party contract services through an ESCO for 52 housing developments. Two ESCOs were selected through competitive bidding processes and tasked with the responsibility to carry out energy efficiency audits in the BC Housing portfolio. Their task included auditing the management of the construction and renovation process, the selection of contractors, and monitoring energy savings (BC Housing 2012). The retrofit program for each development was assessed by the BC Housing Portfolio Management Team using a set of criteria including lifecycle assessment, costs and energy savings to determine the scope of the project. Funding under the HRP provided retrofits to 8338 units, about a third of the 27,000 social housing units currently in the BC Housing portfolio (Interview data, BC Housing Senior Asset Manager, February 2012).

Retrofits in cooperatives and non-profits under federal contracts with CMHC were funded separately. Project submissions were reviewed by a special CMHC committee and went through a complex and vigorous application process that was centrally managed in Ottawa. The CMHC selected eligible projects in BC based on predetermined criteria for a total of $43 million (CMHC 2010). About a third of the applicants received funding. Cooperatives used an intermediary, such as the Provincial Federation of Housing Coops, to prepare project submissions and in many cases to manage the construction process once the project was approved. Once funded, some cooperatives hired project managers to complete contracting and supervision as the deadlines were tight—all work had to be completed by April 2011. Large cooperative providers could supply project management expertise from in-house. Throughout the application and implementation process, cooperatives received support from the federal governing body of housing co-operatives, the Co-operative Housing Federation of Canada (Interview data, Policy Expert, April 2012).

The BC *LiveSmart Efficiency Assistance Program* (LEAP) ran two programs, one managed by a utility company and another by the non-profit association (City Green Solutions 2010). These two intermediaries managed $30 million allocated for energy efficiency retrofits in 1949 units in low-income housing developments. The $2,000 per unit funding cap geared the selection of retrofit measures toward small-scale improvements such as lighting, weatherization, fan replacement and thermostat installation. MEMPR approved applications and decided upon the amount of funding per unit. Housing providers were asked to select the buildings that had a history of poor energy performance. For programs managed by the utility companies, the unit amount could be exceeded on a case-by-case basis. The utility companies also provided matching funds to achieve higher electricity or natural gas savings (interview data, January 2012).

Cash flow was also managed differently based on the presence or absence of a third party. For example, accountability for financing and budgeting was a part of the BC Housing and ESCO contract. BC Housing had discretion over the use of funds and prioritization of types of retrofits. The CMHC was the central administrator and distributor of funds for the cooperative housing program and disbursed the money on the basis of completed works. CMHC personnel were involved in overseeing the management of projects by housing cooperatives and/or non-profit providers through on-site visits. Project managers in some of the larger developments were responsible for procurement of construction works, financing, and reporting to CMHC (Tsenkova and Cliff 2012). In cases where social housing providers did not use a third party, they managed cash flow and implementation themselves within a retrofit plan and with expenses approved by CMHC.

Key informant interviews indicated that housing providers using an intermediary were able to undertake retrofits in a more efficient manner due to economies of scale and a higher degree of professionalism (Interview data, BC Housing Asset Management Team, February 2012). Housing providers who managed funding themselves struggled with staff capacity and the ability to deliver programs effectively and on time. An exception was when building managers had replacement reserve plans, building condition assessments and/or energy audits already in place. Another major difference in the program delivery was the degree to which energy efficiency was a focus of the retrofit. The ESCOs used energy audits to identify and prioritize measures that aligned with the reduction of GHG emission targets (BC Housing 2012). Cooperatives and non-profits funded by the CMHC used energy assessments only if they had applied for and received funding to conduct one. Retrofits for cooperatives were selected first on the basis of critical replacement needs, and second on the best value offered by the energy efficiency retrofits. "Often the lower cost retrofits were not necessarily the most efficient ones." There were very few projects in the cooperative model that solely addressed energy efficiency (Interview data, Policy Advisor, April 2012). *BC LiveSmart* explicitly targeted small-scale energy efficient retrofits with quicker returns. This program is ongoing.

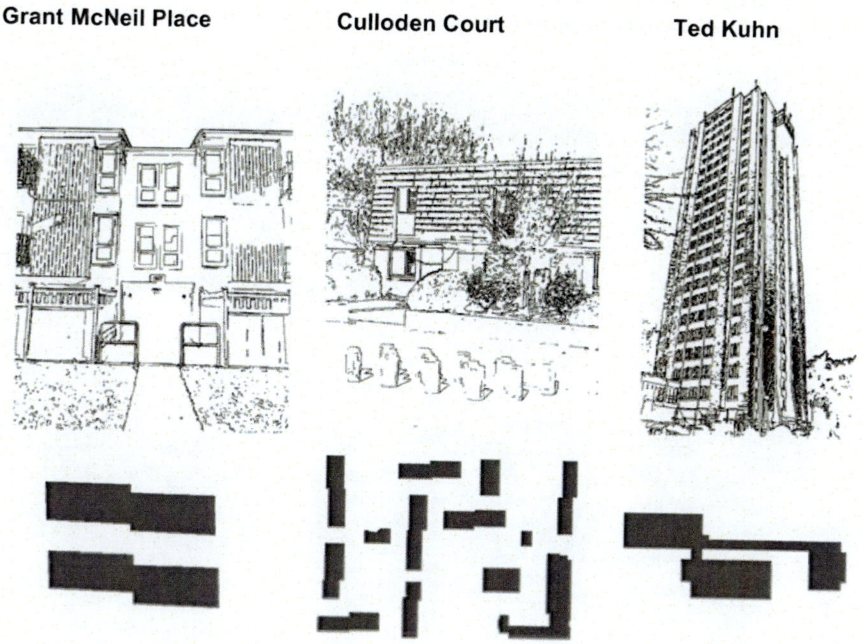

Fig. 3.1 Vancouver case study profiles: Source: Author

3.5 Vancouver Case Studies Overview: BC Housing Projects

Three case studies in Vancouver provide more specific project implementation details. These case studies were chosen to highlight best practices in energy efficiency retrofits from the ESCO model funded by HRP in BC's Housing portfolio. They highlight the types of retrofits and projected feasibility of energy and financial savings. Implementation was undertaken with a combined package of renovation and energy retrofit measures.

The three case studies were Grant McNeil Place, Culloden Court and Ted Kuhn. Grant McNeil and Culloden Court are low- to mid-rise multi-apartment developments serving a mix of singles, seniors and families, whereas Ted Kuhn is composed of two high-rise towers of eight and twenty-one storeys respectively, which provides housing for those transitioning from homelessness (see Fig. 3.1).

All three projects were built between 1969 and 1976. All of the units operated under a rent-geared-to-income (RGI) scheme, where 30% of income was paid to the housing provider in rent and the province subsidizes the remainder. Although exact rental rates were hard to quantify, rents typically ranged from \$400 to \$500 per month depending on the size of the dwelling. Many of the residents did pay utility bills, but the cost of heating was included in the rent.

Table 3.3 BC housing project characteristics

Study Area/Characteristics	Grant McNeil Place North Vancouver, BC	Culloden Court Vancouver, BC	Ted Kuhn Surrey, BC
Year of Construction	1976	1969	1972–1976
Building Type	Low rise apartment	Low rise apartment and townhouse	High rise apartment
Bedrooms	2–4 bed	1–5 bed	Bachelor–2 bed
Storeys	2–3 storey	2 storeys	8 storey and 21 storeys
No. of Units	112 units	132 units	436 units
Total Area	113,832 sq. ft	171,082 sq. ft	243,061 sq. ft
Project economics			
Total Funding Received	3.1 million	3.7 million	11.1 million
Funding Per Unit	RGI	RGI	RGI
Type of Rent	$500/month	$500/month	Under $500/ month
Tenant characteristics			
Tenant Turnover	Very low	Low	Medium–high
Utilities/Heating Included in Rents	Yes	Yes	Yes

Source: BC Housing (2009), BC Housing (n.d.-a, n.d.-b) and Interview data, Capital projects manager, February 2012 (The information in the case study profiles is taken from the feasibility report provided by BC Housing: Ted Kuhn (pp. 4.6, 5.5, 6.3, 7.3), Grant MacNeil (pp. 21, 22, 24–26) and Culloden Court (pp. 58–60)

Tenant turnover in these developments varied. Tenants in Grant McNeil Place and Culloden Court had more stable situations, while Ted Kuhn had a higher turnover based on the transient status of its residents. Ted Kuhn was also the only housing provider with mental health and addiction support staff (Interview data, Housing Manager, February 2012). Tenant turnover affected profitability and financial building operations. If vacancies were frequent and lengthy, less cash was collected in rent (Table 3.3). On the affordability continuum, these projects fall between supportive housing and social housing.

3.5.1 *Types of Retrofits Completed*

Energy assessment performed by the ESCOs identified a comprehensive package of retrofits responding the needs of each development. Many of these included window or door replacement, sealing and caulking to reduce air leakage, replacement of lighting and provision of low flow equipment. Larger retrofit projects were also completed, such as upgrades to space heating, exhaust systems and domestic hot water systems (see Table 3.4).

Table 3.4 Retrofits completed: Vancouver

Retrofits Completed	Grant McNeil Place North Vancouver, BC	Culloden Court Vancouver, BC	Ted Kuhn Surrey. BC
Energy audit performed	X	X	X
Boiler replacement	X		X
Domestic hot water	X	X	X
Solar hot water system		X	
Heat pump (Furnace)		X	
Low flow water fixtures	X	X	X
Water metering	X		
Window replacement	X	X	X
Door replacement	X	X	X
Lighting	X	X	X
CPTED	X	X	X
Common area	X	X	X
Insulation			X
Exhaust upgrade	X	X	X
Mould/asbes-tos removal	X	X	X
Other	Bathtub caulking Fence/balcony replacement	Community centre renovation	Security system
Tenant Feedback			
	Increased comfort Discontent with low flow shower water pressure	Increased comfort Didn't like paying utilities	Increased comfort Issue with windows and automatic fans

Source: BC Housing (2009), BC Housing (n.d.-a, n.d.-b) and Interview data, BC Housing Asset Manager, February 2012

One of the most common retrofits was window replacement, installing double-glazed argon filled windows to improve insulation and temperature control (Fuller 2009; HUD 2011). Grant McNeil Place and Ted Kuhn replaced the domestic hot water heaters and boilers, while Culloden Court was the only development to install solar panels and an accompanying solar hot water pump. Grant McNeil Place also reinsulated ageing piping (Fig. 3.2). It was reported that major systems such as domestic hot water and boilers made the most difference in energy savings, second to window and other insulation (Interview data, Housing manager, February 2012). To some degree all buildings dealt with asbestos and mold abatement due to the use

Fig. 3.2 Illustration of Retrofits: Grant McNeil, Culloden and Ted Kuhn. Source: Interview data, BC Housing Asset Manager, February 2012

of dated building construction methods, poor thermal bridging, and general building lifecycle issues. It is interesting to note that retrofits did not include installation of meters to determine energy consumption (heating) in individual dwellings, thus no incentive was provided to tenants to save energy.

The ESCO-BC Housing contract included the recruitment of a tenant engagement coordinator to inform tenants about the impact of construction on daily living. There were a number of open houses and tenant meetings to keep tenants informed about on-going project activities. In addition, the coordinator was present on-site to address questions or concerns with construction. The major advantages of the mandated public engagement strategy included an improvement to prior BC Housing tenant engagement processes and an enhanced understanding by tenants of the importance and positive effects of retrofits. This helped improve tenant buy-in and supported effective communication between tenant engagement coordinators and construction project managers (Interview data, February 2012). As a result of the retrofits, many tenants reported better comfort due to insulation measures such as door, window and boiler replacements. Those at Grant McNeil Place said they now enjoy more reliable hot water supply. There have been a few complaints regarding the adjustment to automatic systems and thermostat controls. Some tenants disliked the automatic bathroom fans and others did not like the new low flow showerheads due to less pressure.

3.5.2 *Energy and Cost Saving Metrics*

Feasibility studies from BC Housing indicated an overall decrease in projected annual energy and costs saving for each project (BC Housing 2009; BC Housing n.d.) The data provided was in the form of preliminary results and while more complete information was expected, it has not been released.

Table 3.5 Annual costs and energy savings pre- and post-retrofit

Energy and consumption costs	Grant McNeil	Culloden Court	Ted Kuhn
GJ	10,427	8,109	Not reported
kWh	1,061,649	760,332	2,789,020 eKWh
Cost of use ($)	$205,412	$183,960	$274, 174
Energy and cost savings[a]			
GJ	3,981	4,208	Not reported
Energy savings	(38%)	(52%)	Not Reported
kWh	45,118	8,658	Not reported
Tonnes GHG	Not reported	211	404
Cost savings	$71,330	$54,158	$284,296

Source: Feasibility studies GM p. 27, CC p.61, TKT p. 1.2
[a]Projections from feasibility studies

In comparing energy savings, Grant McNeil Place had an annual projected energy savings of 38%, whereas Culloden Court reported a 52% projected reduction (Table 3.5). Cost savings were dependent on the amount of money originally invested and on the type of retrofits implemented. For example, Culloden Court had an original investment of $3.7 million, with annual energy costs savings of $54,158, resulting in a simple cost recovery time of approximately 67 years. This was the longest cost recovery time compared to Ted Kuhn and Grant McNeil Place at 39 and 43 years respectively.[5]

3.6 Vancouver Case Studies Overview: Retrofits in Housing Coops

Data in Table 3.6 profiles two projects in Vancouver that received CEAP funding administered by the CMHC. The case studies were not necessarily representative of the variety of strategies used and the upgrades carried under the program by 31 coops in the city (CHFC 2010). The total allocation was $10.3 million over a two-year period.

Killarney Gardens coop was a large development built in the 1960s with 227 units in townhouses and low-rise apartments. With the support of COHO repair services, members applied for $3.1 million through the CEAP/CMHC program to replace roofs, windows and patio doors. The retrofits were difficult to implement with no tenant relocation. There were significant structural and envelope issues that had to be addressed. Some of the most important retrofits were:

- Double-paned argon filled windows to rectify condensation issues
- Roof replacement and insulation.

Tenants did not pay utility bills separately, but the management was aware of the positive impact on the cost of heating resulting in a significant reduction in the natural gas bill. Management of the coop was proactive and secured funding from *LiveSmart* for smaller, low cost energy efficient retrofits, such as programmable thermostats, shower heads, kitchen aerators and bathroom fans (Interview data, Property Manager, September 2012) (Fig. 3.3).

[5]Calculations for return on investment figures = annual projected cost savings divided by the original investment.

Table 3.6 Coop housing retrofits completed and tenant feedback: BC

Study Area	Four Sisters Housing Co-op Vancouver, BC	Killarney Gardens Housing Co-op Vancouver, BC
Project type and characteristics		
Year of Construction	1987	1960s
Building Type	Low & mid-rise apartment	Low rise apartment & townhouse
Bedrooms	Bachelor–3 bed	1–3 bed
Storeys	4, 5 & 7 storeys	2 & 5 storeys
No. of Units	153 units	227 units
Project economics		
Total funding received	$197,876	3.1 million
Type of rent	30% near market/share purchase	30% RGI & 30% near market/share purchase
Rent	$500–$1,000/month	$800–$1,300/month $2,800–$4,100/family
Tenants		
Tenant turnover	Very low	Very low
Tenants pay utilities	Yes	No
Retrofits completed		
	Retrofit of all external metal works (clean up, treatment, painting).	Roof replacement, patio doors and window replacement
Tenant feedback		
	Extensive involvement of tenants, joint decisions with co-op members to go forward	Managers report high level of tenant satisfaction with new windows, improved thermal and noise comfort and reduction in utility costs.

Source: Interview data, 2011

3.7 Concluding Comments

3.7.1 *Program Successes*

Capital funding through the *Economic Action Plan* and the *BC Housing Renovation Partnership* provided a major opportunity for the implementation of a comprehensive package of retrofits and improvements in the social housing sector. This program was successful in meeting its targets, and accounted for improvements in about 20% of the social housing in the province. As the most significant share was allocated to BC Housing, it was not surprising that the program addressed in a comprehensive manner both energy efficiency and capital improvement needs in the provincial housing portfolio. The majority of the funding, $164 million, was directed

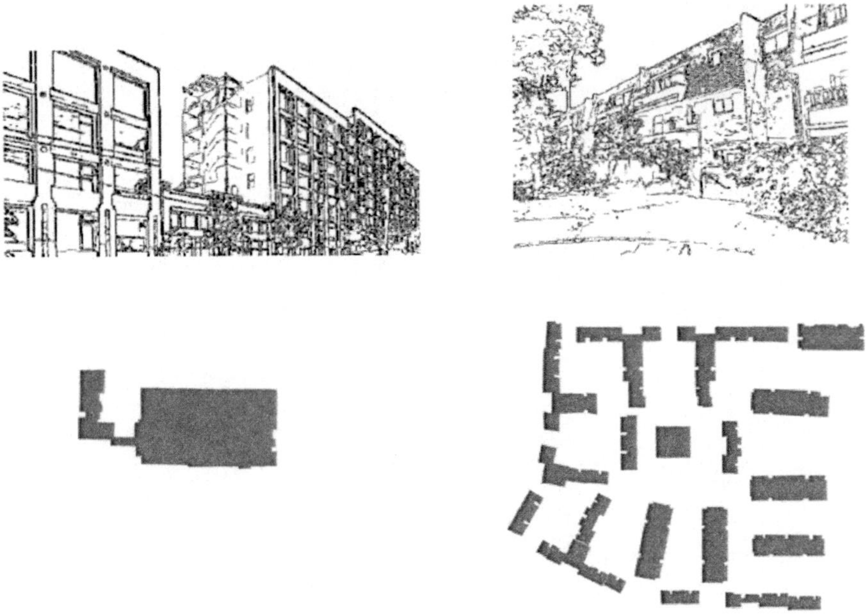

Fig. 3.3 Illustrations of housing coop retrofits: Four sisters and Killarney Vancouver. Source: Author

toward repairs at 84 social housing developments managed by BC Housing and 38 projects by the non-profit housing sector (with over 2000 units). Half of the social housing developments were located in Vancouver, providing affordable housing to households in the greatest need as well as people transitioning from homelessness. One of the major challenges in the program, particularly the component administered by the CMHC, was the decision to tradeoff between energy efficient retrofits and the replacement of deteriorated components. Sometimes there was not enough funding to do both. However, even if retrofits did not incorporate a high level of energy efficiency, energy savings materialized due to the replacement of these components. Overall, the evolution in the social housing system was positive, but not necessarily strategic and the policy design remained limited to 'trial and error' responding to constraints.

CEAP made a substantial difference in the social housing sector in BC, and in Vancouver in particular, given its scale and emphasis on overall building envelope improvements and retrofits of mechanical systems. Interview data indicated that energy and costs savings were a direct result and feedback from tenants was positive. Overall, housing providers believed that the goals of the programs were realized, but it the actual energy saving across the entire portfolio were not determined. BC Housing developed a business model where they partner capital projects with sustainability initiatives from other provincial programs, such as funds for carbon neutral public sector through the *Public Sector Energy Conservation Agreement* (administered through BC Hydro). Nearly $75 million was allocated as capital funding to retrofit existing provincial public sector buildings, including public housing. BC Housing leveraged three different funding sources to maximize the reduction in energy use and GHG emissions of its housing stock, including *BC LiveSmart*. The program had modest targets, but the $2,000 per unit subsidy provided an incentive to introduce measures with quick returns and to engage utility companies in follow-up retrofits.

As these were grant funds, program participants did not attempt to recover costs through rent, but the federal government made it clear that the program was not going to be continued and 'it is a job creation and not a housing program' (Interview data, Senior Policy Expert, February 2012).[6] While provincial programs did provide some funding for maintenance upgrades, the investment needed to support the entire BC social housing portfolio was not addressed. On the institutional side, the programs prompted a more strategic approach to asset management and assessment of both energy retrofit and capital investment needs with major housing providers. The Cooperative Federation in BC developed a partnership with VanCity, a credit union, to provide a combination of grants and low cost mortgages to sustain retrofitting in the cooperative sector. The cooperatives were able to address the tension between short-term affordability goals and the long-term viability of their housing stock through the program, which created a necessity for strategic planning (Interview data, Director, February 2012). This improved governance and decision-making around capital planning projects.

BC Housing reported a similar outcome. The large investment opportunity in the last 3 years increased accountability and fostered new practices in the housing sector's business model (Interview data, Portfolio manager, February 2012). Managing large capital projects raised the credibility of the sector and its capacity to deliver successful retrofit programs. Another critical success factor was the incorporation of the ESCOs in program management at 52 BC Housing properties. BC Housing commissioned an overall assessment of the entire public housing stock, where two ESCOs recommended energy use reduction strategies based on a number of criteria (payback/alignment with provincial criteria for funding programs and carbon credit available from provincial government at $25/tonne). Such evaluations were further refined using a simple ranking system developed by BC Housing to define priority retrofits to be supported through CEAP (see Table 3.7). While the ESCO model was more expensive than the project manager/contract services model used by the coops, there were value-added components including efficiency in program delivery and execution due to economies of scale and expertise, and a 'one stop shop' approach and enhanced accountability for planning, financing and monitoring projects. The partnerships between BC Housing and the ESCOs did signal that small housing providers would benefit from the model and the

[6]Exact data is yet to be released on job creation. A BC government press release reported that 88,000 jobs were to be created through HRP and 1130 jobs were to be created specifically for the energy efficiency retrofits in social housing (Government of British Columbia 2009).

Table 3.7 BC housing priority ranking system

Reported energy reduction measures impacting service plan target	
First priority in measure selection will be given to measures that directly impact Service Plan Target of 5% Reduction in Greenhouse Gas Emissions per year	
Capital renewal measures based on needs of major building systems	
Additional priority in measure selection will be given to capital renewal measures to partner renewal needs with energy reduction measures for management efficiencies. Further energy-use reduction on renewal items can be delivered with a focus different than energy-use reduction	
A	Measures with a high energy-use reduction and quick payback (the "*Cream*")
A−	Measures with a low energy-use reduction and a longer payback (the "*Right-thing*")
B+	Items that cannot be deferred any longer (the "*Required*")
These are measures that are general renewal in nature and may not have any impact to energy-use reduction, but require the expedient resolution offered by the ESCO process	
B	Items that have little energy reduction but are desired (the "*Wishlist*")
These measures are general renewal in nature and may not have any impact to energy-use reduction but make sense to partner with a selected energy reduction measure or are Owner-requested	

Source: BC Housing, Capital Asset Management, Interview data, February 2012

accumulated experience in managing and executing retrofit programs in the future (Lepri 2009).

3.7.2 Program Challenges

Program challenges were associated with tight timelines and difficulties in coordinating and planning strategic retrofits. Although the projects supported through the *Economic Action Plan* were deemed 'shovel ready', housing providers and building managers had to operate within a 2-year timeframe. Unexpected building envelope problems were frequently reported, resulting in cost overruns, project delays and potential loss of funding if projects were not implemented on time (Interview data, April 2012). More flexible deadlines were incorporated into the second round of funding, which alleviated the pressure to retrofit or lose it.

One of the greatest challenges was the high cost of the program and the lack of sustainability in funding. In more comprehensive improvement and energy efficiency projects, such as those in the case studies, payback periods were anywhere between 39 and 67 years. Even though the financial viability and cost-benefit of these programs were not the main objectives, they highlight the future economic challenges. The ESCOs, despite their efficiency, increased the costs and did not function as a mechanism that enhances cost recovery. Rent reforms and other approaches to secure long-term funding and more effective asset management practices would be needed, in addition to strong political motivation to improve the quality and the energy efficiency of the sector.

References

Arman, M., Zuo, J., Wilson, L., Zillante, G., & Pullen, S. (2009). Challenges of responding to sustainability with implications for affordable housing. *Ecological Economics, 68*, 3034–3041.

BC Housing. (n.d.). *Feasibility study report: Grant MacNeil Place. Energy management contract. Internal document*. Vancouver: BC Housing.

BC Housing. (2009). *Comprehensive feasibility study: Ted Kuhn towers. energy management contract. Internal Document*. Vancouver: BC Housing.

BC Housing. (2010a). Canada - British Columbia affordable housing agreement. Retrieved February 3, 2012 from http://www.bchousing.org/aboutus/agreements/CANBC

BC Housing. (2010b). Housing renovation partnership. Retrieved February 3, 2012 from www.bchousing.org/.../Fact_sheets/BCH-Factsheet-HRP-Renovations

BC Housing. (2012). *BCH and ESCO: Implementing the Energy Service Companies (ESCO) briefing notes. Draft Internal Document*. Vancouver: BC Housing.

BC Housing. (n.d.-a). *Feasibility study report: Culloden Court. Energy management contract. Internal Document*. Vancouver: BC Housing.

BC Housing. (n.d.-b). *Feasibility study report: Grant MacNeil Place. Energy management contract. Internal Document*. Vancouver: BC Housing.

Canada Mortgage and Housing Corporation (CMHC). (2001). Healthy high-rise: A guide to innovation in the design and construction of high-rise residential buildings. *Enhancing Energy Performance*. Retrieved March 20, 2012 from http://www.cmhc-schl.gc.ca/en/inpr/bude/himu/hehi/index.cfm

Canada Mortgage and Housing Corporation (CMHC). (2009). *Renovation and retrofit of existing social housing: Provincially/territorially administered renovation and retrofit of existing social housing initiative*. Retrieved November 30 from http://www.cmhc.ca/housingactionplan/reresoho/lipr.cfm

Canada Mortgage and Housing Corporation (CMHC). (2010). *Application guidelines: Renovation and retrofit of existing social housing administered by CMHC*. Retrieved November 30 from http://www.cmhc.ca/housingactionplan/reresoho/index.cfm

Canadian Home Builders' Association. (2011). *Energy use and greenhouse gas emission performance in Canadian homes since 1990: 1990 - 2008 update*. Ottawa: Canadian Home Builders' Association.

CHFC. (2010). *Co-operative Housing Federation of Canada. News Brief, 2010, v. 18 n. 2*. Retrieved February 2, 2012 from http://www.chfcanada.coop/eng/pages2007/news_3.asp

City Green Solutions. (2010). *Strategic energy management plan: Engaging the non-profit housing sector in energy management. Internal report*. Vancouver: City Green Solutions.

Fuller, M. (2009). *Enabling Investments in Energy Efficiency; a study of energy efficiency programs that reduce first-cost barriers in the residential sector*. Berkeley: University of California, California Institute for Energy and Environment.

Government of British Columbia. (2007). *BILL 44 — 2007GREENHOUSE gas reduction targets Act*. Retrieved March 20, 2012 from http://www.leg.bc.ca/38th3rd/1st_read/gov44-1.htm

Government of British Columbia. (2009). Press Release. *B.C., Canada partner to renew social housing*. October 14, 2009. Retrieved March 5, 2012 from http://www2.news.gov.bc.ca/news_releases_2009-2013/2009PREM0050-000481.htm

Hulchanski, D. J. (2004). What factors shape Canadian housing policy? The intergovernmental role in Canada's housing system. In R. Young & C. Leuprecht (Eds.), *Canada: The state of the federation 2004: Municipal-federal-provincial relations in Canada*. Montreal: McGill-Queen University Press.

Lepri, D. (2009). Monthly update newsletter for C.A.M. Group: Energy service company reducing the greenhouse gas emission of the public housing stock. *CAM Times*, May 2009.

Tsenkova, S., & Cliff, C. H. (2012). *Beyond energy efficiency: Investing in social housing in Vancouver*. Paper presented at the ENHR Conference, Lillehammer, Norway, June 23–26.

Tsenkova, S., & Youssef, K. (2012). Canada. Energy efficiency retrofits: Policy solutions for sustainable social housing. In S. Tsenkova, N. Niebor, V. Gruis, & J. van Hal (Eds.), *Energy efficiency in housing management: Policies and practice in eleven countries*. London: Routledge.

U.S. Department of Energy. (2008). *Energy intensity indicators in the U.S.: Efficiency vs. intensity*. Retrieved March 20, 2012 from http://www1.eere.energy.gov/ba/pba/intensityindicators/efficiency_intensity.html

U.S. Department of Housing and Urban Development (HUD). (2011). *Evidence Matters: Transforming knowledge into housing and community development policy. Quantifying energy efficiency in multifamily rental housing.* Retrieved April 8, 2012 from http://www.huduser.org/portal/periodicals/em/summer11/index.html

Chapter 4
Energy Efficiency Retrofits in Social and Affordable Housing in Toronto

4.1 Introduction, Objectives and Methodology

"Energy conservation is the most efficient and effective way for municipalities to reduce energy cost and protect the environment" (Association of Municipalities of Ontario 2012, p. 15). As a part of the 2009 *Canada's Economic Action Plan*, the federal government allocated $352.16 million to the Province of Ontario (ON) to renovate and retrofit the existing social housing stock in the province. The province matched federal funding and distributed the money between the 47 Consolidated Municipal Service Managers, who then selected eligible social housing providers from across their respective portfolios. The aim of the *Social Housing Renovation and Retrofit Program* (SHRRP) was to improve the quality of the housing stock, while helping low-income Canadians and creating opportunities for jobs in construction and related industries.

This chapter investigates the implementation of energy efficiency measures through SHRRP, as well as the CMHC administered renovation and retrofit programs aimed at improving the social housing stock in Toronto. It builds on a literature review of energy efficiency programs for the social housing sector in Canada and the reviews of energy efficiency retrofit policy and practices in British Columbia and Alberta (Tsenkova and Youssef 2012; Tsenkova and Clieff 2012). Given the size of the social housing sector in Ontario and the diversity of institutional arrangements, this chapter focuses on the City of Toronto, and the administration of SHRRP and the Renewable Energy Initiative (REI). Toronto has the largest social housing portfolio in the province with over 90,000 social housing units eligible for funding under SHRRP and REI. The analysis reviews the main programs implemented with a focus on funding mechanisms, implementation criteria, types of retrofits completed and outcomes.

Three case studies from Toronto's social housing portfolio were identified to analyze program implementation and outcomes. These three case studies were selected to represent the renovation strategies of the three major types of social/

S. Tsenkova, *Energy Efficient Affordable Housing*,
https://doi.org/10.1007/978-3-030-69563-7_4

affordable housing providers in Toronto: (1) the local housing corporation—Toronto Community Housing Corporation (TCHC); (2) non-profit housing corporations; and (3) co-operative housing corporations. The selection was also guided by recommendations from the Managers and the project leads from the City of Toronto's Social Housing Unit. Each housing provider agreed to participate in the study.

The methodology builds on literature review, content analysis of major policy documents and case study project information. In addition, 12 key informant interviews and site visits were undertaken in September and December 2012 to develop an understanding of program implementation measure outcomes and on-site challenges/issues related to program management. Specific emphasis was placed on a systematic comparison of the types of energy efficiency retrofits and renovation measures to highlight different investment strategies, as well as to document simple return on investment. Retrofit measures were grouped in three major categories: (1) major mechanical; (2) non-mechanical/building envelope; and (3) renewable energy.

4.2 Social Housing in Toronto

The City of Toronto's social housing portfolio represents approximately one-third of all the social housing in the Province of Ontario (City of Toronto 2001). At the end of 2011, 93,198 units were under management and administration by the City's Social Housing Unit of the Shelter, Support and Housing Administration Division, including 3877 units that are a part of the private rent supplement and housing allowance programs (City of Toronto 2011). Social housing was a significant feature within Toronto's landscape. It provided 29% of all rental units in the City, houses approximately 220,000 people, and played a critical role in the provision of affordable housing services for low-income households since over 70,000 housing units provide rent geared-to-income (RGI) assistance. The waiting lists for social housing (RGI) have grown significantly over time, signalling a high level of need for affordable housing.[1]

The types of social housing organizations managing the social housing stock were: (1) the local housing corporation—Toronto Community Housing Corporation (TCHC)—a non-profit corporation owned by the City of Toronto and governed by a board of directors appointed by City Council,[2] (2) private non-profit housing owned and operated by community based non-profit organizations, (3) and cooperative housing owned and operated by community-based non-profit cooperative

[1]The City of Toronto manages a centralized list, which at the end of 2006 had 67,083 households waiting to access a RGI unit in social housing—about the same number of households already living in subsidized units. Waiting times range from 2 to 12 years, depending on the unit size that a household is eligible for, the rate at which units become available and the length of the waiting list for buildings selected by the household.

[2]Toronto Community Housing Corporation is the country's largest landlord.

Table 4.1 Profile of Social Housing in Toronto, 2007[a]

Program	Total Units	RGI Units	Housing Providers/ Owners
Social/Affordable Housing			
Non-Profit Housing Corporations	20,740	10,401	159
Coop Housing Corporations	7,448	4,789	68
Toronto Community Housing Corporation	58,194	52,429	1
City Developed Non-Profit Projects	832	660	13
Sub-Total	*87,214*	*68,279*	*241*
Market Housing[b]	3,665	2,690	9
Total	*90,879*	*70,969*	*250*

Source: Adapted from City of Toronto (2007)
[a]Data refers to housing under City administration as of December 31, 2006
[b]Market housing includes private housing under rent supplement, housing allowance pilot and limited dividend housing

corporations, whose members are residents of the cooperative (City of Toronto 2012). TCHC owned and operated 63% of the social housing stock. The remainder of the social housing in the City was provided by 250 non-profit and cooperative housing organizations (City of Toronto 2011).[3]

A profile of Toronto's social housing portfolio is presented in Table 4.1. With the exception of TCHC, only three of the housing providers operate more than 500 units, while most operate a single building with fewer than 200 units. Several studies assessing the physical condition of the City's social housing stock found that the buildings were generally in good condition, but that most housing providers would not have sufficient funds to meet their future capital repair needs such as roof repairs, and mechanical and electrical systems upgrades (City of Toronto 2001, 2011). The

[3]In January 2001 and May 2002, the City of Toronto, along with the other municipalities in Ontario, assumed the administration and funding responsibilities of the social housing programs previously funded and administered by the federal and provincial governments. The *Social Housing Agreement* (SHA), which was signed in November 1999, initiated the transfer of administrative responsibilities. The SHA was an agreement between the Ministry of Municipal Affairs and Housing (MMAH) and the CMHC. The agreement required the transfer all federal responsibilities for social housing programs to the Province of Ontario, with the exception of the federal cooperative housing program which continues to be funded and administered by the CMHC. Following the SHA was the *Social Housing Reform Act* (SHRA) in 2000, which required municipalities to assume responsibility for the funding and administration of social housing programs from the Province and/or the CMHC. The SHRA was completed in two stages. In stage one of the transfer, ownership, funding and administrative responsibilities of the public housing stock (then known as the Metro Toronto Housing Authority, now known as the Toronto Community Housing Corporation) was transferred to the City of Toronto, which administers its Service Manager role through the Shelter, Support and Housing Administration Division. In stage two of the transfer, responsibility for the remaining social housing programs was transferred to the City. As a result, 95,350 units, including community non-profit, non-profit cooperative, and the City's municipal non-profit housing corporation units, are now under the administrative and management of the City of Toronto (City of Toronto 2001).

TCHC reported immediate capital repair needs of $751 million (2012 dollars), stating that failure to make these investments would result in the withdrawal of housing units due to the failure to meet an appropriate standard for occupancy (City of Toronto 2007). As the capital repair backlog increased each year, the TCHC projected capital needs over $ 1 billion by 2012 in the absence of new sources of funding (Bailão et al. 2012). The report on the non-profit and cooperative social housing portfolio indicated that to meet future capital repair needs, funding of capital reserves should be increased by $34 million annually. Reports to Council pointed out a significant financial exposure and risk to the City for unfunded future capital repair needs (see City of Toronto 2007 for additional discussion of these issues). The physical condition of the social housing portfolio and the lack of adequate reserves to address capital needs, as well as the limited institutional capacity of some small community based non-profit organisations to undertake complex retrofit programs, affected the implementation of the SHRRP.

4.3 Funding Programs and Mechanisms

In 2009, the federal and the provincial government of Ontario launched a number of policy initiatives and capital grant programs to support energy efficiency retrofits in social housing. In addition to improving the condition of existing social housing and tenants' quality of life, these efforts were aimed at stimulating job creation and reducing energy consumption and impacts on the environment (Tsenkova and Youssef 2011). The policy tools and initiatives are discussed below.

4.3.1 Social Housing Renovations and Retrofit Program

The SHRRP was a capital grant program formed under the *Canada-Ontario Housing Initiative*. The federal and provincial governments jointly funded the SHRRP with Ottawa contributing $352.16 million through the *Renovation and Retrofit of Existing Social Housing Initiative* (part of the CEAP), with Ontario contributing the remaining funds to support its *Poverty Reduction Plan*. A total of $704 million was available in the 2009–2011 fiscal years (City of Toronto 2009a). Eligible social housing programs included:

- Public housing projects developed by the Ontario Mortgage and Housing Corporation (formerly the Ontario Housing Corporation) and transferred to service managers under the *Social Housing Reform Act* (SHRA);
- Projects under the SHRA and formerly funded under federal/provincial non-profit housing programs (non-profit and cooperative housing) and unilateral provincial non-profit housing programs (non-profit and co-operative housing);

- Projects developed under the federal Section 95 housing program including the Urban Native Housing Program; projects developed under the Section 26 housing program (including the Limited Dividend Program) and the Section 27 housing program directly funded by the CMHC; and
- Off-reserve projects funded under the Rural and Native Housing Rental Program (Ministry of Municipal Affairs and Housing 2009).

The Ministry of Municipal Affairs and Housing used notional fairness principles to distribute the funds to the 47 consolidated municipal service managers in Ontario. They received a share of the $704 million corresponding to the relative share of social housing in their service area. If the service manager administered 30% of the total social housing units in the province, they received 30% of the funding available. Service managers had authority within the parameters of the published Provincial Guidelines, to distribute funds to social housing providers (Interview data, Provincial Program manager, August 2012). This simple rule ensured some fairness in the distribution of funds across the province and left the service managers sufficient autonomy to address priority needs.

The City of Toronto is one of the 47 service managers in Ontario. Over a 2-year period, the SHRRP provided approximately $220 million to the City for construction ready capital repair projects in the social housing sector (City of Toronto, Shelter, Support and Housing Administration 2009a, b). The SHRRP funding was an indispensable investment to improve the state of social housing in the city, and was consistent with the direction of *Housing Opportunities Toronto* and the City's *Ten Year Affordable Housing Action Plan*. The SHRRP funding also reduced the impact of the withdrawal of federal and provincial funding resulting from the social housing transfer in 2002, and therefore was a necessary investment to fund capital repairs required for exiting social housing across the province. The three key priorities of the SHRRP were to: (1) improve the health and safety of tenants; (2) increase the energy efficiency of buildings; and (3) increase building accessibility for seniors and persons with disabilities (Ministry of Municipal Affairs and Housing 2009). The two categories of capital projects permitted under the program were renovation and retrofit projects and regeneration projects.

4.3.2 *Federally Administered Retrofit Program*

Retrofits in cooperatives and non-profits under federal contracts with CMHC were funded separately. Project submissions were reviewed by a special CMHC committee and went through a complex and rigorous application process that was centrally managed in Ottawa. The CMHC granted $40.5 million to eligible projects in Ontario based on predetermined criteria (CMHC 2010). About a third of the applicants received funding. Cooperatives used an intermediary, such as the Provincial Federation of Housing Coops, to prepare project submissions and in many cases to manage the construction process once the project was approved. Once funded,

Table 4.2 Capital program investments in the social housing sector: Ontario and Toronto

Program	Funding Source	Amount invested	Projects
CEAP Renovation and Retrofit of Existing Social Housing Initiative	Economic Action Plan/Housing Renovation Partnership	$704million ($220 million in Toronto)	5817 housing developments (includes city owned, non-profit housing and coops) (~2500 projects in Toronto)
CEAP Renovation and Retrofit of Existing Social Housing Cooperatives	Economic Action Plan/CMHC	$40.5 million ($6.0 million in Toronto)	299 coops (48 projects in Toronto)
Renewable Energy Initiative	MMAH	$70 million ($30.6 million in Toronto)	NAV (92 projects in Toronto)

Source: CMHC (2012); Interview Data, Program Director, September 2012

some cooperatives hired project managers to complete contracting and supervision as the deadlines were tight. All works had to be completed by April 2011. Large cooperative housing providers had in-house project management expertise, while others received support from the Cooperative Housing Federation of Canada (Interview data, Policy Expert, April 2012). Nearly 300 projects received grants for renovation and energy efficiency retrofit work in Ontario, and about 16% of these projects were located in Toronto (see Table 4.2). Grants were relatively small and covered specific measures such as the replacement of heating systems and windows, and improvements to the units.

4.3.3 Renewable Energy Initiative

In 2010 the Ministry of Municipal Affairs and Housing (MMAH) provided $70 million in federal and provincial funding to further facilitate social housing renovation and retrofit initiatives (City of Toronto 2010b). As a one-time funding opportunity, the *Renewable Energy Initiative (REI)* was aimed at further reducing operating costs for housing providers by installing renewable energy technologies for heating, cooling and/or generating electricity. Specifically, the program supported investment in: (1) solar photovoltaic (roof top systems); (2) solar water heating; (3) solar air heating; (4) geothermal; and (5) mid-sized wind technologies (City of Toronto 2010b). The Province required that contractors for REI supply and installation be from an approved vendor of record list. The list was administered by the Ontario Power Authority.

Council approved applications were submitted for potential renewable energy projects by the Shelter, Support and Housing Administration. The Province awarded $30,672,243 as a conditional allocation under the REI for 59 projects from the TCHC portfolio ($21,396,674) and 33 projects from the non-profit and cooperative housing provider portfolios ($9,275,569) (City of Toronto 2010b). Funding allocation was based on compliance with program requirements, regional fairness across the province, and a balanced distribution of technology implementation.

4.3.4 Toronto Community Housing Corporation Retrofit Initiatives

The TCHC has faced many challenges in managing the largest share of social housing in Toronto, most of it in delivering RGI housing assistance, but has also initiated a number of programs to enhance tenant quality of life. SSHRP and REI funding allowed these efforts to be scaled up and implemented in a more efficient manner. The TCHC had the ability to raise funds directly due its AA class debt rating from Standard and Poor, which has allowed borrowing from capital markets to fund redevelopment projects such as Regent Park and Don Mount Court, as well as to address backlogs in capital repairs.[4] Some of the TCHC initiatives prior to the launch of SHRRP included:

- Building Renewal Plan: $100 million, 4-year investment in 19 communities
- Neighbourhood revitalization: $7 million to open and renew community spaces, playgrounds, community gardens and sports facilities to enhance community safety
- Energy Efficiency: a partnership with Brahms Energy Saving Team to reduce energy consumption in their community through energy-saving light bulbs, by saving $17,000 in energy costs and winning *the 2006 Green Toronto Award for Community Initiative*
- Appliance Replacement: replacement of fridges, stoves, showerheads, toilets and furnaces with energy efficient models, saving over $1.2 million, reducing energy consumption by 3% across the portfolio and winning *2006 NRCAN Energy Star of the Year Award*
- Unit Refurbishment Program: $75 million invested to upgrade about 9,000 bathrooms and kitchens (and related unit mechanical systems) to improve unit interiors.

Because of the size of its social housing portfolio, the TCHC had the ability and the capacity to benefit from different programs and emphasised the importance of energy and water savings by installing energy and water efficient systems and devices. The TCHC had a large asset management team, manages its own Building Renewal Energy program to fund such measures from its capital reserve fund and set up a project management clearing house—Housing Solutions Inc.—to oversee a more holistic approach to renovation and energy efficiency retrofits. The entity was a

[4]In 2007, TCHC placed a $250 million bond to address capital repairs and redevelopment needs. Interviews suggest that the TCHC may have exhausted its current debt servicing capacity.

subsidiary of TCHC managing many retrofit projects (Interview Data, Asset Management Team, September 2012). While the greening of social housing had many benefits, the installation of "green" technologies was a strain on capital reserves, some with a lengthy payback.[5]

4.4 Program Implementation Results

4.4.1 Institutional Framework

Administration of SHRRP funding was structured around an Administration Agreement between the City and the Province. This agreement served to outline the partnership between the Province and the City by specifying the principles, requirements and procedures guiding reporting, payments and the creation of funding agreements for projects. City staff was also responsible for ensuring that the SHRRP guidelines and reporting requirements were met through the verification of invoices and financial statements submitted by housing providers, and by undertaking site visits. Since the monitoring of the program required staff resources, the Province committed additional funding to offset administrative costs over the 2 years of program administration (City of Toronto 2010a).

Figure 4.1 shows the institutional framework for social housing investment initiatives by federal, provincial, and municipal government in the City of Toronto. The City of Toronto was the Service Manager, through the Shelter, Support and Housing Administration Division (SSHA). With City Council approval, this department was responsible for administering the SHRRP program, including the distribution of funds and monitoring of projects. In the 2-year period the staff working on SHRRP ranged between 4 and 9 people with asset management experts involved at the start of project submission, review and approval. The present staff was extensively involved in monitoring, site inspections, advice and capacity building on capital planning, particularly for some of the small housing providers. City staff was also instrumental in initiating audits for small housing organizations and promoting holistic thinking about the building and retrofit cycle (Interview data, Program Manager, September 2012). Some of the funded projects specifically targeted energy efficiency measures as City staff placed them in the category of 'big utility spenders' to ensure that unsustainable high utility bills were addressed through retrofit measures. Once funding was approved, all projects were self-managed by the individual housing providers and contractors were chosen on the basis of a tendering process. The SSHA reported to City Council and MMHA on program results, disbursement of funds and general metrics of performance.

[5]The Housing Services Corporation has been working for several years to deliver its Energy Management Program, which assists smaller social housing providers with green retrofits. Funds come from the Ontario Power Authority, Toronto Hydro and other utilities.

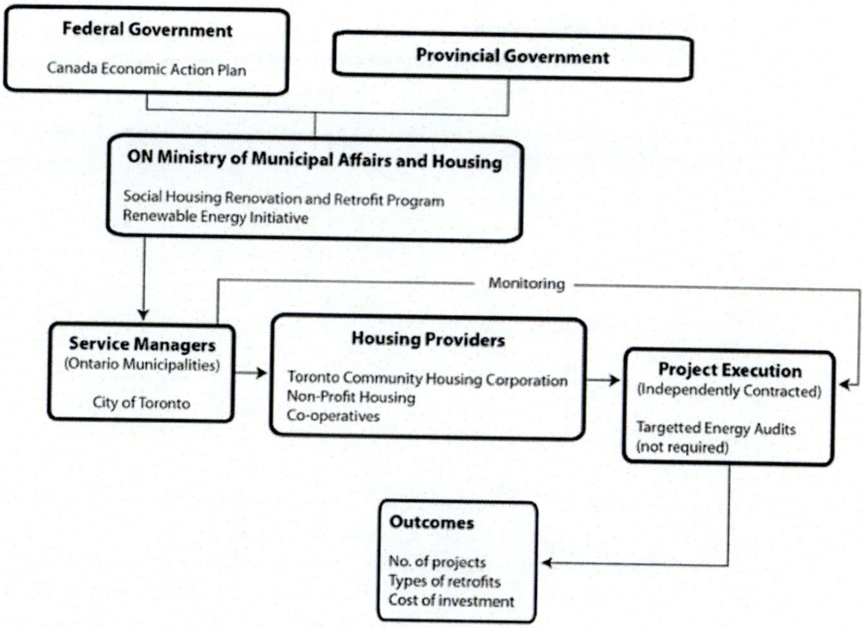

Fig. 4.1 Institutional framework of social housing renovation and retrofit programs in Toronto. Source: Author

4.4.2 Metrics of Performance

For both the SHRRP and the REI, the City of Toronto Council authorized the Shelter, Support and Housing Administration to submit projects on behalf of the City to the MMAH, and to subsequently allocate funding to the TCHC, non-profit and cooperative housing providers. For each project approved by the Province for funding, the City and Province entered into a *Provincial Funding Agreement*. Upon execution of the agreement, the Province transferred 20% of the project funds to the City (City of Toronto 2009b). Upon the commencement of construction, 50% of the funding was forwarded, and the remaining funds were transferred when the project reached 90% completion (City of Toronto 2009b). The City as program administrator disbursed the funds to housing providers through a *Provider Funding Agreement* upon completion of specified project milestones.

The total SHRRP allocation of $259 million had a significant impact on the social housing portfolio in Toronto. The TCHC received the largest share (58%), followed by the non-profit housing providers (31%). In terms of the impact measured by the number of units affected, the TCHC improved over half of its portfolio with SHRRP funds, while units in the non-profit and coop sector accounted for 34% and 11% of the total. However, a comparison of these statistics against the number of units managed by non-profits and coops in the City (see Table 4.3) revealed that every non-profit and coop housing provider received funding and support to upgrade over

Table 4.3 SHRRP and REI funding allocations and impact

Proportion of SHRRP and REI funding allocated				
	SHRRP		*REI*	
TCHC	$150,688,073	58%	$21,396,674	70%
Non-Profits (other than TCHC)	$79,841,232	31%	$5,797,272	19%
Cooperatives	$28,505,246	11%	$3,478,297	11%
Total	$259,034,551	100%	$30,672,243	100%
Proportion of units impacted by SHRRP and REI				
	SHRRP		*REI*	
TCHC	32,419	55%	7645	70%
Non-Profits (other than TCHC)	19,924	34%	2200	20%
Cooperatives	6,610	11%	1152	10%
Total	*58,953*	*100%*	*10,997*	*100%*

Source: Interview Data, Program Manager, City of Toronto, September 2012

90% of the units in their portfolios. It did not seem that notional fairness allocation of funds was a management objective, rather City staff worked hard to ensure that smaller organizations were successfully included. The allocation model used to distribute the REI funding was based on submissions from each social housing provider (refer to Table 4.3). The data indicated that REI funding supported more TCHC projects, perhaps due to its institutional capacity to absorb grants and the existing management structure that had promoted retrofits and the use of renewal energy features since 2006.

Although the administration of the program was complex, the City of Toronto's SSHA efficiently managed the process. As a result, there was an overall increase in the number of projects submitted for funding in the second year. In the first year, 109 social housing providers were approved for funding with TCHC accounting for 70% of all the projects, whereas in the second year this number increased to 178 housing providers (City of Toronto 2010a). Due to more staff resources, sufficient time to recruit consultants, and effective collaboration and communication with the social housing providers, program opportunities were maximized. The number of smaller housing providers in the non-profit and cooperative sectors that received funding from 2010 to 2011 increased substantially to 55% of the total (City of Toronto 2010a).

4.5 Toronto Case Studies

Three case studies were chosen to comparatively analyze SHRRP program implementation in Toronto. The case studies represented retrofit strategies by the three main housing provider types in Toronto: (1) non-profit; (2) cooperative; and (3) the local housing corporation. The case studies also highlighted best practice in energy efficiency retrofits under the SHRRP program. The first section profiles the projects,

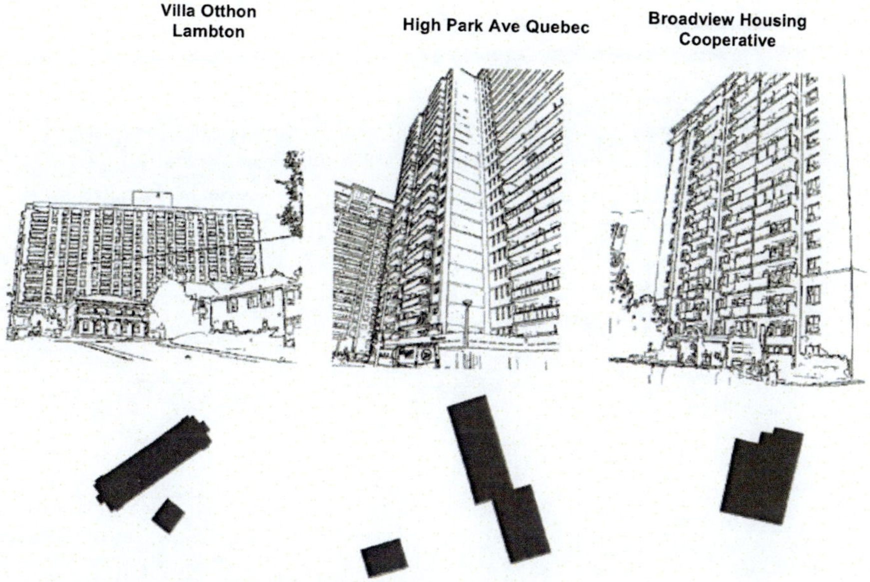

Fig. 4.2 Case Studies in Toronto. Source: Author

followed by an overview of the types of retrofits implemented and estimated energy and cost savings. Figure 4.2 presents case study characteristics such as location, building type and building footprints.

Villa Otthon, Broadview Housing Cooperative and High Park Quebec were residential towers ranging from 11 to 24 storeys in height. Villa Otthon and High Park developments also included a small town house complex. The buildings were built between 1969 and 1989. All the units had controlled market rents, with 60–100% of the tenants receiving RGI housing assistance. Monthly market rents typically ranged from $800 to $1,200 depending on the size of the unit. Residents did not pay utility bills and the cost of heating and hot water was included in the rent. Tenant turnover was an issue in Villa Otthon due to the comprehensive retrofit measures required in the units. The project took 18 months to complete and initially met with a great deal of tenant opposition (Interview data, Building Manager, September 2012) (Table 4.4).

4.5.1 *Types of Retrofits Completed*

Audits completed for each housing developed identified key retrofits that responded to the specific needs of each development. City staff used these studies to identify potential projects for SHRRP support. Mechanical upgrades, such as the replacement of heating systems, makeup air units and cold-water booster pumps, accounted

Table 4.4 Toronto housing project characteristics

Study area	Villa Otthon Lambton	High Park Quebec	Broadview Housing Cooperative
Year of Construction	1989	1965, renovation in 1997	1969
Building Type	Residential Tower/Townhouse Complex	Residential Tower	Residential Tower
Bedrooms	1–3 bed	1–3 bed	Bachelor–3 bed
Storeys	11	15	24
No. of Units	194 apartments (+6 under construction in Year 1)/8 Townhouse	111 apartments	449 apartments
Project Economics			
Total SHRRP Allocation	$3,937,164	$700,753	$2,175,049[a]
Funding Per Unit	$18,929	$6,313	$4,844
Type of Rent	65% RGI 1b.$1,000; 2b.$1,200 Townhouse $1,400	60%RGI 1b-$900; 2b. $1,110	90% RGI 1b.$850; 2b.$1,200
Average Rent	NAV	NAV	$1,651
Tenant Characteristics			
Tenant Turnover	Medium (21 units vacant)	Very small	Medium
Tenant Pay Utilities	No	No	No

Source: Interview data, 2012b and 2012c

[a]SHRRP funding was offered on a "use it or lose it" basis. Under the SHRRP rules, if the funding was not used or approved projects were not completed within the fiscal year, funds would be reallocated to other projects by the MMAH. The original amount requested and approved for the High Park development under the SHRRP program was $3,992,229. As a result of reallocation, the actual funding was $2,175,049

for the majority of the investment, whereas non-mechanical upgrades such as general repairs to building facilities and replacement of appliances represented the smallest percentage of project investment (Table 4.5).

Retrofits related to renewable energy technology were the solar thermal installations in Villa Otthon and Broadview, accounting for 2% and 32% of project costs. Lighting improvements, as well as the installation of low flow toilets and water conserving showerheads, were implemented in High Park. These different types of projects demonstrate different priorities. For example, the replacement of the electric heating plant with a gas-fired heating plant in Villa Otthon did cost $2.9 million, but was prompted by a disproportionately high bill for heating and utilities that exceeded $400,000/per year. The new system used natural gas, which resulted in a major reduction in utility bills (Interview data, Building manager, September 2012).

Figures 4.3 and 4.4 illustrate some of the major retrofits implemented in the case study projects. Initiatives supporting the retrofits included:

Table 4.5 Retrofits completed

Type	Villa Otthon	Broadview	High Park[a]
Renewable Energy	*2%*	*32%*	
Solar Thermal System	$60,000	$225,196	
Mechanical	*81%*	*55%*	
Makeup Air Units[b]	$110,000	$15,617	X
Heating Plant (boilers and conversion)	$2,944,757	$215,408	X
Cold Water Booster Pumps	$40,000	$85,728	
Building Automation Controls	$75,000	$69,144	X
Non-Mechanical	*7%*	*1%*	
General Building Upgrades[c]	$165,793		
Audits[d]	$8,065	$4,061	X
Unit Kitchen & Bathroom Upgrades[e]	$96,879		X
Other Costs	*11%*	*12%*	*X*
Total SHRRP Allocation (100%)	*$3,937,164*	*$700,753*	*$2,175,049*

Source: Interview data, Program Manager, City of Toronto and Building Managers, September 2012

[a]Data on the cost of individual project components are not available for High Park

[b]The Makeup Air Unit category also includes garage ventilation

[c]The General Building Upgrades category also includes replacement of balcony panels, elevator room repairs, paint and signage upgrades, lighting upgrades, pipe rehabilitation (corrosion control), and backflow prevention device installation

[d]The Audits category also includes asbestos audit and abatement (in the case of Villa Otthon), building condition audits and capital reserve fund forecast

[e]Unit Kitchen and Bathroom Upgrades category includes appliance replacement, low flow toilet installation and water conserving showerhead installation

Fig. 4.3 Major retrofits at Villa Otthon. Source: Author's field work, 2012

- Staff training to ensure efficient use and maintenance of new systems;
- Communication strategies to articulate renovation and retrofit plans and the potential benefits to building tenants, and
- Occupant behavioral change programs to encourage energy responsible behavior, especially in buildings where tenants are not responsible for individual utility costs (Interview data, Building Managers, September and December 2012).

Fig. 4.4 Major Retrofits at Broadview Housing Cooperative. Source: Author's field work, 2012

In Villa Otthon, management constructed two mock up apartments to demonstrate the impact of the retrofit measures. This was particularly helpful in addressing tenant concerns. Building managers worked proactively to minimize the disruption caused by construction work in the building and had ongoing support from City staff. Tenants reported high levels of satisfaction with the improvement measures and appreciated the tangible benefits to common areas in the buildings.

4.5.2 Energy and Cost Saving Metrics

Energy Audits and feasibility studies conducted prior to the implementation of renovation and retrofit projects projected an overall decrease in energy consumption resulting in cost savings for each case study. The data provided in Table 4.6 represents these preliminary estimates. Post retrofit studies were required to confirm the impact on actual energy consumption of projects supported by the social housing retrofit and energy efficiency initiatives.

With respect to energy savings, Villa Otthon had an annual projected estimate of 37% in savings, Broadview projected an estimate of 27% in savings, and the High Park development projected an estimate of 16% in savings. The projected energy cost savings exceeded $100,000 for Vila Otthon and High Park. These estimates included energy retrofit incentives provided by Enbridge Gas and the City of Toronto's Building Better Partnerships, as well as rebates offered by Ecoenergy in Ontario (Finn Projects 2009a, b).

In addition to the economic benefits of reducing energy use, the feasibility studies claimed significant environmental gains resulting from reduced consumption of water and GHG emissions. For example, a reduction of 295 tonnes of GHG was equivalent to growing 7565 tree seedlings for 10 years, or taking 54 passenger cars off the road for a year. Such gains were impressive, given the fact that in two of the projects the GHG reduction was twice and three times the projected amount.

Table 4.6 Projected annual costs and energy savings

Energy and consumption costs pre-retrofit	Villa Otthon Lambton	Broadview Housing Co-operative	High Park 100 High Park Ave	High Park Quebec
Electric kWh	3,062,123	962,425	2,862,827	127,911
Gas cu.m.	235,135	284,021	801,240	1
Water cu.m.	N/A	N/A	81,803	1
Cost of use ($)	$455,373	$210,636	$724,608	$17,734
Energy and Cost Savings Post-retrofit[a]				
Electric kWh	1,675,176	184,484	221,062	24,117
Gas cu.m.	−57,124	91,451	217,076	0
Water cu.m.	N/A	N/A	3,449	0
GHG Reduction	296	772	455	5
Energy Savings	37%	27%	16%	19%
Cost Savings	$168,244	$56,949	$118,594	$3,344

[a]Projected
Source: Source: Finn Projects (2009a, b) and Ameresco Canada Inc. (2009)

As with the research completed in British Columbia and Alberta (Tsenkova and Clieff 2012; Tsenkova and Youssef 2011), the return on investment was dependent on the amount of capital, energy cost savings, and types of retrofits implemented. For example, Broadview had an original investment of $611,093 for mechanical retrofits with a projected annual energy savings of $26,815.

Table 4.7 presents the simple payback period of these measures, ranging from 19 to 68 years (in the case of solar thermal systems). In comparison, Villa Otthon invested $3,229,975 for mechanical retrofits, contributing to energy savings with a simple payback period of 7–77 years (in the case of the heating plant). Collectively these measures projected annual energy savings of $63,300. The data remain limited, as the non-mechanical upgrades also affect building envelope insulation and may reduce energy and water consumption.

4.6 Regeneration Projects and Design Innovation

4.6.1 42 Hubbard Boulevard: TCHC Regeneration Project

Under the SHRRP, service managers were permitted to use up to 10% of the total 2-year funding allocation to fund regeneration projects. In the second year of the SHRRP, the TCHC requested $4,050,000 for regeneration of the Hubbard Boulevard development. The building was 80 years old and in need of significant repairs and retrofits to improve the performance, functionality and accessibility of the units. In 2008, during kitchen and bathroom repairs, TCHC determined that the building could not be maintained due to major renovation requirements to remediate mold, asbestos, and other safety issues.

Table 4.7 Costs and payback of SHRRP funded energy retrofits

Broadview housing co-operative mechanical—energy retrofit description	*Cost*	*Projected annual energy savings*[a]	*Anticipated simple payback*
Make-Up Air Units	$15,617	$7,059	2.2
Heating Plant	$215,408	$10,993	19.6
Solar Thermal System	$225,196	$3,298	68.3
Cold Water Booster Pumps	$85,728	$3,265	26.3
Building Automation Controls	$69,144	$2,200	31.4
All SHRRP Retrofits	*$700,753*		
Villa Otthon Mechanical—Energy Retrofit Description	*Cost*	*Projected Annual Energy Savings*[a]	*Anticipated Simple Payback*
Make-Up Air Units	$75,000	$11,700	6.4
Heating Plant (boilers and conversion)	$2,944,757	$38,000	77.5
Solar Thermal System	$60,000	$3,900	15.4
Cold Water Booster Pumps	$40,000	$2,600	15.4
Garage Ventilation	$35,000	$2,600	13.5
Building Automation Controls	$75,000	$4,500	13.6
All SHRRP Retrofits	*$3,937,164*		

[a]Gas savings only (does not include electricity savings) are used in the simple payback calculations
Source: Finn Projects (2009a, b); Ameresco Canada Inc. (2009); Interview data, Program Manager, September 2012

The social housing development is adjacent to the boardwalk in the Beaches, one of the most attractive historic neighbourhoods in downtown Toronto, and is itself a historic resource. The building contributes to the character of the neighbourhood and provides an opportunity to integrate social housing tenants in a high-income area. During the reconstruction, only the original façade of the 3-story, 27-unit property was preserved. In addition to the installation of an elevator and other accessibility features, the primary goal of the regeneration was to meet a 40% efficiency improvement and create a new amenity area for tenants (Toronto Community Housing 2012a, b).

The interior was completely rebuilt with original stained glass windows and other historic elements incorporated in the new design. The emphasis on sustainability and simplicity in design is remarkable and certainly defines the unique attributes of this development (Interview Data, project Architect, September 2012). The regeneration was completed in January 2012 and the building is fully occupied. The total cost of the regeneration was $5,894,340, and it provided 27 apartments. SHRRP funding and other energy efficiency and regeneration resources were used to cover project costs. Summary of the costs is presented in Table 4.8. This one-of-a-kind regeneration project had a significant price tag with costs of $210/sq ft, close to the $230/sq ft cost of newly built housing. Half of the original tenants were able to come back to Hubbard Boulevard and live in RGI housing units. The other 18 apartments had market-based rents, ranging from $1,200 to $1,500 per month. These rent levels were reportedly half of what true market rents would be in the Beaches area (Interview Data, Project manager, September 2012).

Table 4.8 Project costs for 42 Hubbard Boulevard

Description of Works	Cost
General Site Costs	$388,750.00
Construction Management	$120,000.00
Architecture & Engineering	$400,000.00
Landscaping	$30,000.00
Earthwork/Shoring/Demolition	$837,680.00
Concrete/Masonry/Structural Steel	$876,350.00
Rough Carpentry/Framing/Gypsum	$865,650.00
Roof/Green Roof/Roof Anchors	$266,600.00
Windows/Exterior Doors/Curtain Wall	$227,910.00
Plumbing/HVAC/Controls/Sprinklers	$831,700.00
Electrical Service/Communication/Security	$538,200.00
Elevator	$98,500.00
Solar PV	$50,000.00
Building Automation System	$113,000.00
Contingency	$250,000.00
Total Expenses	*$5,894,340.00*

Source: Interview data, Project manager, September 2012

Box 4.1 42 Hubbard Boulevard—Energy Efficiency by Design SHRRP funding and other energy incentive programs offsetting the cost of energy efficiency and renewable energy measures allowed for new design features, including:

- Insulation and new windows to make units more comfortable and to reduce heating costs
- Energy efficient heating, air conditioning, and lighting
- Rooftop solar panels to generate electricity
- A green roof to improve aesthetics, building cooling, and rain water management
- A building automation system to fine tune energy use.

Source: Interview Data, 2012

4.6.2 Solar Walls

Through SHRRP funding, four Toronto housing providers installed solar air heating systems. SolarWall© air heating is a renewable energy technology developed in Toronto. SolarWall© systems are typically wall-mounted (although modular rooftop systems—SolarDuct©—are also available) and can be designed to cover an entire wall or to blend into windows and other architectural details on a wall. SolarWall© resembles a traditional metal wall cladding system. The exterior is comprised of a specially perforated collector installed 6–12 in. from the exterior wall, creating an air cavity. It acts as the ventilation air-intake for the building. Fresh air is heated as it passes through the perforations in the system and the heated air is collected in the air cavity behind the wall, where it is directed into the building's HVAC system. The solar heating reduces the energy load on the conventional heater (City of Toronto 2011) (Fig. 4.5).

Three TCHC projects in Moss Park used REI funding to install SolarWalls© (275, 285 and 295 Shuter Street). Two towers installed two wall-mount systems totaling 3,388 sq ft, which should offset over 85 tonnes of CO_2 each year. A rooftop system was installed on the third tower. The choice was prompted by the fact that SolarWalls© provide a renewable energy technology blending both solar pre-heated air and heat recovery from suite ventilation, while reducing energy consumption. The SolarWall© heating system was most affordable and the payback was high when installed as part of a cladding replacement project. In the Harry Sherman Crowe Housing Cooperative at York University Campus, the systems were installed on a wall covering 6,400 sq ft. These systems were heating 18,000 cfm of air for the building, and provided energy savings of over $15,000 each year. The systems were expected to offset over 130 ton. of CO^2 each year.

Fig. 4.5 SolarDuct© and SolarWall© Air Heating Systems. Source: Author's field work, 2012

4.7 Concluding Comments

The renovation and retrofit programs were successful in achieving the goals of improving the quality of social housing in Ontario, reducing energy costs, and improving the overall condition of the housing stock. Nearly 300 projects received grants for renovation and energy efficiency work in Ontario, and about 16% of those were located in Toronto through the CMHC administered program. In the SHRRP program, the Ministry of Municipal Affairs and Housing used notional fairness allocation to distribute funds to the 47 consolidated municipal service managers in Ontario that received a share of the $704 million corresponding to the relative share of social housing in their service area. This simple rule ensured some fairness in the distribution of funds across the province and left the service managers sufficient autonomy to address priority needs. In the City of Toronto the investment was critical in addressing the lack of resources needed to fund capital repairs and system upgrades in the aging social housing stock. The capital shortfall for social housing in Ontario was estimated at $2 billion. The City of Toronto reports to Council highlighted significant financial exposure and risk to the City for unfunded future capital repair needs. The physical condition of the social housing portfolio and the lack of adequate reserves to address capital needs, as well as the limited institutional capacity of small community based non-profit organisations to undertake retrofit programs, affected the implementation of the SHRRP.

Interviews consistently pointed out that without the combined funding from SHRRP and REI, most of these retrofits would not have materialized. The issues were particularly critical for small social housing providers in the non-profit and co-op sector that did not have the capacity to raise funds for critical upgrades, nor necessarily the institutional expertise to deal with complex retrofit programming and budgeting operations. In terms of overall impact, SHRRP provided grant funds for a variety of mechanical, structural and building envelope improvements affecting two thirds of the social housing portfolio in Toronto. The impact, in terms of units upgraded, was particularly significant for the non-profit and co-operative housing providers, which saw over 90% of their portfolio affected by program measures. The capital investment enabled the renovation and retrofit of nearly half of TCHC social housing, including comprehensive energy efficiency projects through SHRRP and REI funding as well as innovative demonstration projects. As the largest social housing provider in the City of Toronto, and indeed in Canada, the TCHC received over 55% of the funding (over 70% of REI).

Part of the City of Toronto's success was attributed to the institutional framework established to manage funds in an effective and efficient manner. City staff worked hard to overcome the constraints of a decentralized model of social housing providers to ensure that program benefits were available to all. Efforts included capacity building, assistance with project submissions, project co-ordination and in some cases commissioning audits to ensure greater response rates in year two of the SHRRP and REI program cycle. Constant monitoring, site inspections, advice and training ensured consistency between planned and actual program measures. Some of the most popular retrofits, in addition to lighting—'the low hanging fruit'—were mechanical system upgrades (boilers), roofing, window replacement and cladding/insulation (Interview data, Manager and project lead, September, 2012).

Some of the challengers were associated with the tight deadlines and the need to quickly identify shovel ready projects, when a systematic approach based on building and energy audits would have been more beneficial. City staff continued to oversee disbursement of SHRRP funds, reallocated for other measures or reassigned across the portfolio (Interview data, Program management team, September 2012). Some of these issues were related to the diverse institutional landscape of social housing providers in Toronto—some social housing providers with the institutional capacity to undertake major projects, and others in need of significant assistance in managing these projects. Program management was stressful and program administration absorbed significant City staff time. Despite these constraints, the approach was strategic and integrated energy efficiency considerations with capital need improvements.

The specific retrofit measures in the case studies were diverse and illustrated the significant challenges of such programs in economic terms. If the simple payback of energy efficiency measures was used as an overall consideration for return on investment, it would have been difficult to make the case for green retrofits in the social housing sector. Feasibility studies, however, pointed to significant environmental benefits resulting from reduced energy and water consumption, and reduced GHG emissions. Some of these metrics of performance, as well as the social impact measured in tenant satisfaction and improved health and well being, were difficult to measure. The largest social housing provider in Toronto (TCHC) emphasised the importance of energy and water savings by installing energy and water efficient systems and devices. While the greening of social housing had many benefits, the installation of green technologies was a strain on its capital reserves. REI provided an important financial boost to experimentation with sustainable design and green technologies such as solar walls/roofs and green roofs, which could become mainstream in the future.

Regardless of the overall success of the programs, the funding only temporarily addressed the lack of resources available to maintain the social housing stock. A longer term and consistent funding model should be developed to ensure the sustainability of results achieved.

References

Ameresco Canada Inc. (2009). *Toronto Community Housing Corporation: Building energy renewal program investment grade feasibility study for High Park Quebec Development*. Toronto, ON: Ameresco Canada Inc.

Association of Municipalities Ontario. (2012). *Energy conservation should be first priority*, Retrieved October 11, 2012 from http://www.amo.on.ca/wcm/AMO/AMO_/AMOAdvocacy.aspx?issue=Energy

Bailão, A., Purves, B., Redway, A., & Pimblett, J. (2012). *Putting people first. Transforming Toronto community housing*. Toronto: City of Toronto Council Report, September.

Canada Mortgage and Housing Corporation (CMHC). (2010). *Application guidelines: Renovation and retrofit of existing social housing administered by CMHC*. Retrieved November 2012 from http://www.cmhc.ca/housingactionplan/reresoho/index.cfm

Canada Mortgage and Housing Corporation (CMHC). (2012). *Canada's economic action plan: Renovation and retrofit of existing social housing*. Retrieved from http://www.cmhc.ca/housingactionplan/reresoho/lipr.cfm

City of Toronto. (2001). *Social housing transfer plan*. Toronto: City of Toronto Administration.

City of Toronto. (2012). *Social housing unit*. Retrieved from http://www.toronto.ca/housing/social_housing/index.htm

City of Toronto, Shelter, Support and Housing Administration. (2007). *Tied in knots: Unlocking the potential of social housing communities in Toronto*. Retrieved from http://www.toronto.ca/legdocs/mmis/2007/cd/bgrd/backgroundfile-8980.pdf

City of Toronto, Shelter, Support and Housing Administration. (2009a). *Economic stimulus funding investments in social housing renovation and retrofit*. Retrieved from http://www.toronto.ca/legdocs/mmis/2009/cc/bgrd/backgroundfile-21365.pdf

City of Toronto, Shelter, Support and Housing Administration. (2009b). *Update on the social housing renovation and retrofit program*. Retrieved from http://www.toronto.ca/legdocs/mmis/2009/cd/bgrd/backgroundfile-24902.pdf

City of Toronto, Shelter, Support and Housing Administration. (2010a). *Social housing renovation and retrofit program. – Allocation of year two funds*. Retrieved from http://www.toronto.ca/legdocs/mmis/2010/cd/bgrd/backgroundfile-26593.pdf

City of Toronto, Shelter, Support and Housing Administration. (2010b). *In year budget adjustment for economic stimulus renewable energy investments in social housing: shelter, support and housing administration*. Retrieved from http://www.toronto.ca/legdocs/mmis/2010/ex/bgrd/backgroundfile-33034.pdf

City of Toronto, Social Housing Unit. (2011). *Toronto social housing by the numbers*. Retrieved from http://www.toronto.ca/housing/social_housing/pdf/shbynumbers.pdf

Finn Projects (Synchronicity Projects Inc.). (2009a). *Building energy audit for broadview housing co-operative: 1050 Broadview Ave*. Toronto, ON: Finn Projects.

Finn Projects (Synchronicity Projects Inc.). (2009b). *Building energy audit for Villa Otthon – Lambton: 40062 Old Dundas St. W*. Toronto, ON: Finn Projects.

Ministry of Municipal Affairs and Housing. (2009). *Canada-Ontario affordable housing initiative: Social housing renovation and retrofit program (SHRRP)*. Retrieved from http://www.mah.gov.on.ca/AssetFactory.aspx?did=6867

Toronto Community Housing. (2012a). *42 Hubbard Boulevard*. Retrieved from http://www.torontohousing.ca/market_rent_buildings/southeast_toronto/hubbard_42

Toronto Community Housing. (2012b). *42 Hubbard Boulevard*. Retrieved from http://www.torontohousing.ca/investing_buildings/42_hubbard_blvd

Tsenkova, S., & Clieff, C. (2012). *Retrofitting BC social housing for energy efficiency: A review of policy and practice in Vancouver*. Calgary: University of Calgary, Faculty of Environmental Design.

Tsenkova, S., & Youssef, K. (2011). *Green and affordable housing in Canada: Investment strategies of social housing*. Calgary: University of Calgary, Faculty of Environmental Design.

Tsenkova, S., & Youssef, K. (2012). Canada. Energy efficiency retrofits: policy solutions for sustainable social housing. In S. Tsenkova, N. Niebor, V. Gruis, & J. van Hal (Eds.), *Energy Efficiency in housing management: Policies and practice in eleven Countries* (pp. 209–231). London: Routledge.

Chapter 5
Renovation and Retrofits of Social Housing in Alberta

5.1 Introduction and Methodology

Housing was a priority on the agenda of the Province of Alberta, with a target of 11,000 new social housing units to be built by the end of 2012.[1] That target was paralleled by efforts to renovate and retrofit existing social housing built 30–40 years ago (Alberta 2011; MHUA 2011). "Building stronger communities starts with housing first" (interview data, Minister of Urban Affairs, November 7, 2011). The Province of Alberta provided a total of $42.4 million to housing management bodies and service providers to support housing stock upgrades, matched by the federal government. Overall, over 700 renovation projects were completed, benefiting more than 20,000 units (interview data, Program supervisor, May 2012). The $84.5 million in retrofit funding supported the repair or replacement of major building components including roofs, windows, heating, and plumbing (MHUA 2011).

The objective of this chapter is to review the results of the 2-year CEAP program targeted at upgrading the social housing stock in Alberta, particularly in its largest cities—Edmonton and Calgary. The research methodology included a literature review to identify main retrofit categories, content analysis of policy documents related to program administration at the federal and provincial level, profiles of select case studies in Edmonton and Calgary, and site visits and key informant interviews. Eight categories of retrofits were used as a broad framework for comparison of the work implemented:[2] (1) window and door replacement, (2) heating system upgrade, (3) roof work, (4) interior modernization, (5) flooring, (6) landscaping, (7) lighting, and (8) other.

[1]As of September 2011, the Government of Alberta is on track to achieve this goal as 11,636 social housing units have been supported through the program (9035 newly constructed units and 2601 purchased/renovated units); 3424 units were constructed in 2011 (http://municipalaffairs.gov.ab.ca/units_target_achieved.cfm).

[2]See Weia and Liu (2017) for specific definitions.

S. Tsenkova, *Energy Efficient Affordable Housing*,
https://doi.org/10.1007/978-3-030-69563-7_5

Table 5.1 Social housing Portfolio: Alberta

	Edmonton	Calgary	Alberta
Social Housing Units	9300	8645[a]	26,500
Percentage of Total	35%	33%	100%
HMB[b]	15	14	130

[a]City of Calgary (2011), p. 41
[b]Based on data from http://housing.alberta.ca/522.cfm

A list of housing service providers (cooperatives and non-profit housing corporations) and housing management bodies (HMBs)[3] who received CEAP funding was reviewed to select the organisations receiving the largest amount of funding, often corresponding to a large share of retrofitted units. This led to a stratified sample of case study projects to represent comprehensive intervention in the public, non-profit and cooperative sector in Calgary and Edmonton. Six projects were profiled to complement a general overview of CEAP program performance for funds administered by: (1) The Ministry of Housing and Urban Affairs (a joined provincial-federal program); and (2) CMHC (a federal program). Housing providers and HMBs were asked to 'self-select' retrofit projects that they deemed representative of program implementation work.[4] Although the sample was small to represent the work carried out in over 700 retrofit projects across Alberta, the main objective of the research was to provide an overview of investment strategies used by different housing providers and to illustrate best practices.

In addition to the case studies chosen, 15 key informant interviews were undertaken to get a better sense of challenges and opportunities in the implementation of retrofit measures. Informants were selected based upon their key role in the decision-making and administration of CEAP funds, as well as in the actual implementation of renovation and retrofit strategies. Interviewees included program supervisors, program analysts, executive directors, board directors, managers, corporate representatives, and information officers.

5.2 Social Housing Portfolio

In 2009 Alberta had 26,500 social and affordable housing units in 1,100 sites that were funded by the federal and provincial governments, as well as 14,000 units supported by provincial rent supplements. Of the 26,500 units, approximately 8,645 units were in Calgary and 9300 were in Edmonton (see Table 5.1). All units were managed by 130 local housing management bodies (HMBs) on behalf of the

[3]HMBs in Alberta manage housing owned by the Alberta Social Housing Corporation. They are established by Ministerial Order under the *Alberta Housing Act*. There are 53 HMBs in the province for family housing and 110 HMBs for seniors housing (AUMA 2012).

[4]In the case of the Greater Edmonton Foundation, the case study profiled is selected to represent the diversity of retrofits and other building envelope improvements.

province. Additionally, 36 non-profit organizations managed special needs housing, which was also eligible for repair funding (MHUA 2011). Although official data on the overall condition of the housing stock was lacking, recent reports highlighted the challenges associated with the deteriorating condition of social housing, particularly in the public sector (Auditor General of Ontario 2009).

5.3 Policy Framework for Energy Efficiency Retrofits in the Social Housing Sector

The Government of Canada and the Government of Alberta partnered on a joint investment to build new and renovate existing affordable housing. Both levels of government officially signed an amendment to the *Canada–Alberta Affordable Housing Program Agreement* and announced $386 million over 2 years beginning in March 2009 for affordable housing (CMHC 2009). The stimulus was intended for projects that were 'shovel-ready' with the expectation that work was complete by March 2011. While there was a formal extension by the Prime Minister of the CEAP infrastructure stimulus fund until December 2011, the social housing projects were considered 'on-schedule' as far as the funds administered by CMHC were concerned, but CEAP funds continued to be administered by the provinces, including Alberta, 2 years after the deadline.

The four main objectives of the *CEAP Renovation and Retrofit Initiative* were to:

- Address the demand for renovations and general improvements,
- Address the need for energy efficiency upgrades,
- Address the accessibility needs for persons with disabilities, and
- Create jobs (CMHC 2010).

In Alberta, the program was administered by a department in the Ministry of Housing and Municipal Affairs that worked directly with HMB on projects submissions, approval and disbursement of funds. The Ministry does not have specific guidelines or priorities to complement the federal guidelines and priorities, but has considered requests for building envelope improvements, measures addressing safety and accessibility, replacement of heating and ventilation systems and other specific energy efficiency retrofits (Interview data, Director, November 2012).

CEAP funds administered by CMHC had specific Canada-wide guidelines and standardised procedures. Eligible repairs and renovations included the following:

- Major building components: roofs, exterior wall finishes, exterior doors and windows,
- Major building services: heating systems and boilers, hot water tanks, circulating pumps and air handling systems,
- Basic facilities: kitchen facilities such as stoves, refrigerators, sink and faucet installation, countertops and cabinets; bathroom facilities such as toilets, sinks and other fixtures,

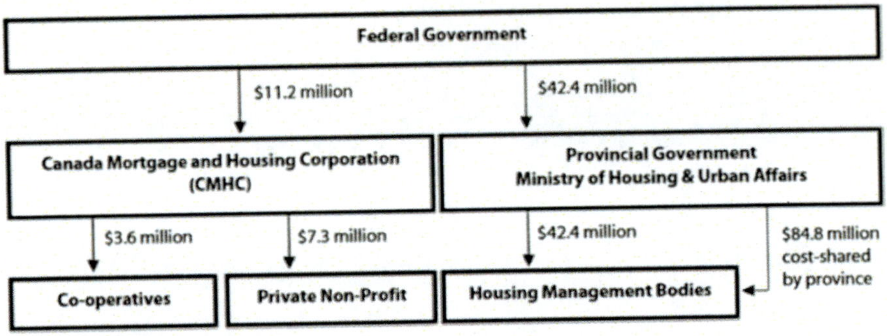

Fig. 5.1 Institutional framework for program administration. Source*:* Author

- Safety features such as fire alarm systems, emergency lighting and intercom systems, and
- Other major facilities, equipment and features such as parking, flooring, garbage disposal systems and other items such as foundations, plumbing systems and emergency generators (CMHC 2010).

Priority was given to housing providers with well-managed housing stock and $4,500 per unit or less in their replacement reserves. Priority was also given to renovations and retrofits that included major critical building systems and services, such as roofs, windows, doors, exterior building envelopes, heating systems, plumbing, electrical and ventilation, as well as those renovations that were required for the health and safety of residents and/or modifications for the disabled. In general, renovations of individual components were required to meet minimum energy standards. For example, window replacement using double paned Low-E Argon windows, roof replacements involving the use of attic insulation to a minimum of R-40, and replacing appliances with Energy Star-rated products (Alberta Energy Efficiency Alliance 2010). Renovations and repairs were not required to result in a specific overall energy rating unless the work was specifically intended as an energy retrofit.[5]

5.4 Policy Implementation

The institutional framework for CEAP program management is presented in Fig. 5.1. All of the projects were self-managed by housing providers and HMBs with general monitoring and control exercised by the Ministry and the CMHC-Prairies Office.

[5]Energy retrofit work is required to result in the unit meeting provincial or territorial energy efficiency standards, based on the age of the building. For example, a low rise building constructed in 1970 would be expected to achieve an Energuide rating equivalent to a range of 63–72. Existing high-rise buildings would be expected to be more energy efficient than the Model National Energy Code for Buildings (see CMHC 2010, 2011, 2012 for additional information).

Table 5.2 CEAP social housing retrofit program results in Alberta

Province/ City	Funds allocated (Federal $M)	Funds allocated (Provincial $M)	Total funding (Provincial & Federal $M)	Projects (not necessarily the number of Housing Management Bodies	Units
Alberta	$42.43	$42.43	$84.86	747	20,827
Edmonton	$13.78	$13.78	$27.56	169	7,774
Calgary	$16.48	$16.48	$32.96	164	7,005
Rest of Alberta	$12.17	$12.17	$24.34	414	6,048

Source: Ministry of Housing and Urban Affairs, Interview data, November 2012

Table 5.3 CMHC social housing retrofit program results in Alberta

Province/ Territory	Cooperative housing		Non-profit Housing		Total[a]	
	Funds ($million)	Projects	Funds ($million)	Projects	Funds ($million)	Projects
Alberta	$3.60	33	$7.30	80	$11.20	122
Edmonton	$1.82	12	$3.02	31		
Calgary	$1.01	6	$4.05	40		

[a]Total funds and total projects includes Urban Native Housing
Source: CMHC (http://www.cmhc-schl.gc.ca/housingactionplan/reresoho/lipr.cfm)

Contractors were chosen based on a tendering process, following standard procurement guidelines for public works. The disbursement of funds was done on the basis of invoices for completed retrofits and renovation items included in the project approval document (Interview data, Senior Program Administrators, November, 2011).

Data in Tables 5.2 and 5.3 provide essential metrics of performance and program results. Provincially administered program funds were allocated to 747 projects and impacted over 20,827 units. Two thirds of these units are in Edmonton and Calgary, with the largest share of funding allocated to the two largest HMBs in the province: the Capital Region Housing Corporation (CRHC) and the Calgary Housing Corporation (CHC).The CRHC in Edmonton managed municipally owned and non-profit projects, and received $17.4 million. The CHC managed municipal and non-profit projects, and received $22.4 million.[6] In the non-profit sector, the Greater Edmonton Senior's Foundation received the largest amount of funding, $3.7 million (Interview data, Program Director, November 2012). Federally administered program funds of $11.2 million also targeted coops and non-profit providers in the two largest cities in the province.

[6]The Calgary Housing Company also received $2.7 million from the CMHC for family housing upgrades (Interview data, Senior Partnership Consultant, April 2012).

Fig. 5.2 Edmonton case study profiles: Father Hannas and Synergen Coop. *Source: Author*

5.5 Edmonton Case Studies Overview

Three case studies were chosen in Edmonton—two supported through CEAP provincially administered funds, and one housing cooperative supported through CMHC administered program funds. The profile presented below follows the approach outlined in the analytical framework (Fig. 5.2). Table 5.4 highlights key characteristics of the housing development, data on project economics and types of retrofits implemented.

5.5.1 *Types of Completed Retrofits*

The Capital Region Housing Corporation utilized *CEAP Renovation and Retrofit* funding to complete the following work at various sites in Edmonton[7] (CRHC 2012):

- Kitchen cabinet replacement in over 150 units,
- Furnace replacement in over 150 units,
- Flooring replacement in over 800 units,
- Re-roofing, and
- Upgrading attic insulation to approximately 3500 units.

[7]Window replacement was undertaken on one site: Tipaskan I (CRHC 2012).

Table 5.4 Edmonton housing project characteristics

Study area	Capital region housing corporation Edmonton, AB	Greater Edmonton Foundation Father Hannas Apartment Building	Synergen housing cooperative
Location	Edmonton, AB	10809 70 Ave NW Edmonton AB	428 Richfield Rd NW Edmonton, AB
Year of Construction		1972–1995	late 1970s
Building Type	Townhouses and apartment buildings	Apartment buildings	Townhouses
Bedrooms		Bachelor/1 bed	
Storeys		3 storeys	2 storeys
No. of Units	Over 5000 units	43 units	44 units
Project Economics			
Total SHRRP Allocation	$17,407,843	$580,800	$660,349
Funding Per Unit	$3,121	$13,507	$15,008
Type of Rent	RGI	RGI	RGI
Average Rent	$516/month	$500/month	Under $500/month
Tenant Characteristics			
Tenant Turnover	Very low	Low	Medium–High
Tenant Pay Utilities	Yes	Yes	Yes

Source: Interview data, CRHC Manager of Property Assets, November, 2011; Interview data, CHC Executive Director, May 2012; CMHC 2012

The choice to use the funding across the portfolio was strategic, prompted by the need to provide building envelope improvements as well as retrofits of mechanical systems. Preference was given to measures aligned with the general lifecycle needs replacement, rather than those targeting energy savings. The work resulted in substantial improvement in terms of safety, quality and standard in half of the units across the portfolio. Close to 7% of the funds were set aside as a reserve for future investment. There were plans to monitor energy savings in one apartment building to identify financial return on investment, but there was no long-term planning for energy efficiency due to the lack of guaranteed funding from provincial and federal governments as well as the high cost of implementing high-tech solutions (Interview data, Manager of Property Assets, November 2011). The CRHC did not carry out energy audits prior to commencement of renovation/retrofit work. Nevertheless, a target of a 20% reduction of energy consumption was set.

Table 5.5 Retrofits completed: Edmonton

Retrofits completed	Capital region housing corporation	Father Hannas apartment building (% of total investment)	Synergen housing cooperative
Window/Door Replacement	X	33%	X
Heating system	X		X
Roof work	X	34%	
Interior modernization	X	4%	
Flooring	X	13%	
Lighting/ electrical		4%	X
Other	X	12%	X
Total investment	$17,407,843	$580,800	$660,349

Source: Interview data, CRHC Manager of Property Assets, November 2011; Interview data, Executive Director, May 2012; CMHC (2012)

The Greater Edmonton Foundation for Seniors improved 1606 units (96%) of its portfolio, implementing a range of renovations and retrofit measures (Interview data, Executive Director, May 2012). The renovations of some buildings, such as Porta Place (73 units) were focused on interior and HVAC upgrades, while in Virginia Park (140 units) and in Canora Gardens (98 units) the focus was on elevator modernization. Projects also included electrical and lighting upgrades, which did not amount to a considerable portion of the budget. Father Hannas Apartment building, profiled in Table 5.4, was a notable exception with a relatively comprehensive retrofit that included roof and window replacement as well as lighting upgrades. In general, the Greater Edmonton Foundation had to make tough investment decisions. Its housing portfolio consisted of buildings that are 30 years old. Management states that they need an additional $10 million to address all issues. Despite the tight frame for program implementation, there was sufficient time to plan, tender and complete the retrofit work. Nevertheless, there were scheduling and construction challenges, and an extension of the time period to cover two consecutive summer seasons would have made implementation much more feasible (interview data, Executive Director, May 2012).

Table 5.5 provides an overview of the types of retrofits completed in the case studies with some indication of costs per component, depending on data availability.

5.6 Calgary Case Studies Overview

Three case studies in Calgary illustrate program results. Two of the housing projects were implemented by CHC, supported through CEAP provincially administered funds, and one of the developments was a housing cooperative funded through CMHC administered program. Figure 5.3 highlights key characteristics of the housing development, data on project economics and types of retrofits implemented (Table 5.6).

5.6.1 *Types of Retrofits Completed*

The case studies illustrated an emphasis on renovating major building components: doors and windows, heating systems, hot water tanks and air handling systems. Other improvements included new kitchen and bathroom facilities, elevators, and safety features. Energy efficiency measures were not explicitly targeted, although the renovation of building and service components might reduce heating costs and energy consumption. Table 5.7 summarizes the retrofits completed in the three case studies. In Baker House, the first priority was window and door replacement, followed by interior modernization (elevator, kitchen and laundry refurbishment) and access for the disabled (Interview data, Project Manager, April 2012). The window replacement recycled existing bronze metal window frames while replacing the glass panels as a cost reduction measure. Funds used for interior modernization were also considerable accounted for 20% of total funds. The high rise building

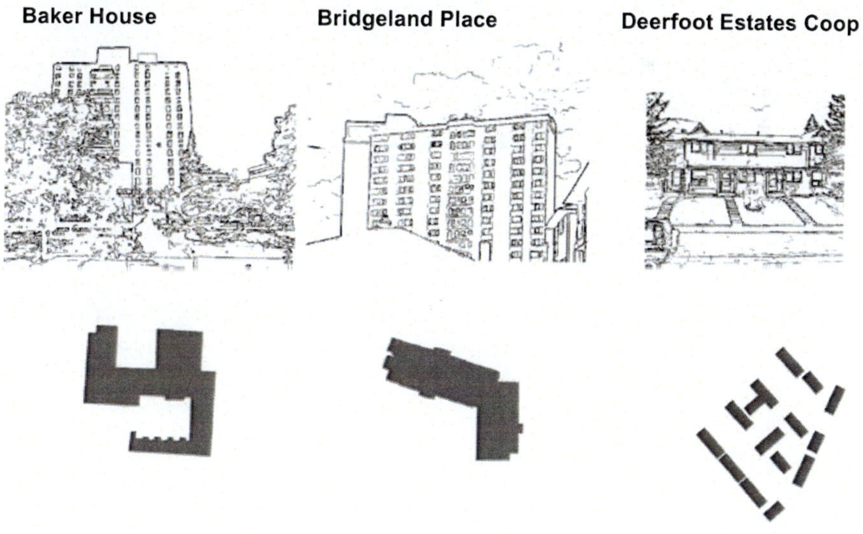

Fig. 5.3 Calgary case study profiles: Source: Author

Table 5.6 Calgary housing project characteristics

Study area	Calgary Housing Company Baker House	Calgary housing company bridgeland place	Deerfoot estates housing co-op
Location	Edmonton, AB	10809 70 Ave NW Edmonton AB	428 Richfield Rd NW Edmonton, AB
Year of Construction	1971	1971	
Building Type	High rise apartment	High rise apartment and townhouse	Townhouses
Bedrooms	173 bachelor, 39 1-bed, 1 2-bed	75 1-bed, 135 2-bed	2, 3, 4-bed[a]
Storeys	16 storey	18 storey	2 storey
No. of Units	213 units	210 units	72 units
Project economics			
Total SHRRP Allocation			
Funding Per Unit	$1,987,120	$1,147,352	$211,628
Type of Rent	$9,329	$5,464	$2,939
Average Rent	RGI	RGI	No subsidy
Tenant characteristics			
Tenant Turnover	Very low	Low	Low
Tenant Pay Utilities	No	No	Yes

Source: Interview data, CHC Portfolio Manager, April 2012; Interview data, Coop coordinator, October 2012

[a]Information available at: http://www.sacha-coop.ca/PDFs/Co-ops/DeerfootEstates.pdf

Table 5.7 Retrofits completed: Calgary

Retrofits completed	Baker House (% of total investment)	Bridgeland Place (% of total investment)	Deerfoot estates housing cooperative
Window/Door replacement	35%	71%	
Heating system	14%	19%	100%
Interior modernization	34%		
Flooring	5%	6%	
Landscaping	7%	3%	
Lighting/ Electrical		1%	
Other	5%		
Total investment	$1,987,120	$1,147,352	$211,628

Source: Interview data, CHC Portfolio Manager, April 2012; Interview data, Coop Co-ordinator, October 2012

housed low-income tenants, and the rent revenue did not allow for the accumulation of reserve funds to carry out much-needed life cycle replacement of building envelope elements and service systems. Other renovations were still needed, despite major improvements resulting from CEAP grant funds. Tenants did not pay for heating costs, and even if individual controls were installed in the units to regulate room temperature, there was no real incentive to use them (Interview data, Project Manager, April 2012).[8]

In Bridgeland Place, another high-rise project in CHC portfolio housing families and seniors, window and door replacement absorbed almost three-quarters of the budget, followed by upgrades to the heating system (boiler, radiator fins, and valves) that absorbed 19% of the budget.

The third case study was a non-profit housing cooperative, the Deerfoot Estates, whose overall strategy was to replace inefficient furnaces in all units, and to replace the hot water tanks in 66 of those units. Digital thermostats were also installed. These measures reduced the energy bill by 50% (Interview data, Co-ordinator, October 2012). The federal funding allowed the cooperative to proceed with comprehensive energy retrofits (for example, the cost of a furnace was $2,179 and that of a hot water tank—$695). Additional fees were incurred to handle issues related to program management, including fund disbursement by CMHC, and issues with contractors (Interview data, Co-ordinator, October 2012).

5.7 CEAP Renovation and Energy Retrofit Program Results

5.7.1 Federal-Provincial Cost-Matched Projects

CEAP funds were invested to improve the building envelope, mechanical and electrical systems of the social housing stock in Alberta, as well as to enhance its quality through interior modernisation, safety and accessibility measures. The program supported 747 projects impacting over 20,827 units, which was over 80% of the social housing in the province.

Although the HMBs made different choices depending on capital needs and servicing requirements across their portfolio, most of the CEAP funding was allocated for window/door replacement (20%), followed by interior modernization (14%) and roof work (10%). Heating and lighting system upgrades targeted specific energy efficiency measures, accounting for 10% of the total CEAP budget (see Table 5.8). Return on investment from energy savings did not seem to be a decisive factor in retrofit choice. The decisions were driven by the need to improve building envelope and service systems and to ensure better quality housing through a range of

[8]The baseboard radiators were controlled via a dial on the fins. Several floods resulted when water pipes burst.

Table 5.8 CEAP renovation/retrofit spending by category in Alberta

Category	Funding ($million)	Percentage of total (%)
Window/Door replacement	$16.72	20
Heating systems	$6.08	7
Roof work	$8.55	10
Interior modernization	$12.05	14
Flooring	$6.67	8
Landscaping	$1.66	2
Lighting/electrical	$2.30	3
[a]Other	$30.83	36
Total Spending	$84.86	100

Source: Ministry of Housing and Urban Affairs, Interview Data, Senior Program manager, November 2012

[a]Other includes elevator modernization, plumbing, pavement and sidewalk upgrades, along with exterior upgrades

renovation measures. What generally characterized the case studies profiled in Edmonton and Calgary was the improvement of the building condition and interior space for tenants in such a way that tenants 'feel' the difference. Thus, less emphasis was placed on energy efficiency retrofits while the achievement of other program objectives were a priority, such as general renovations and improvements in safety and quality of social housing. Some of these measures, such as replacement of windows, roofs and insulation, no doubt had an impact on energy consumption and reduced energy costs. The CEAP funding was timely and allowed the HMBs to replace building and servicing components in their aging building stock that had reached, or were very close to reaching, the end of their life-cycle.

Despite the challenging time frame for completing retrofit work, large HMBs were in an advantageous position compared to smaller cooperatives and non-profit organizations in terms of their institutional capacity to administer funds, and therefore accounted for the largest share of program funding.

5.7.2 *Federally Funded Projects*

A total of 2043 cooperative and non-profit housing units in Alberta were retrofitted in year one (62% in Calgary; 34% in Edmonton), while 1,275 units (61% in Calgary; 28% in Edmonton) and 152 beds (75% in Edmonton) benefited from renovations in year two. Half of the cooperatives in Alberta received funding. Nine cooperatives received $1.3 million in funding in year one, of which 65% went to three coops in Edmonton and one coop in Calgary. Of the $2.2 million funding in year two, 90%

Table 5.9 Type of retrofits supported through CMHC funds

Type of retrofit work	No. of projects	No. of units	No. of beds
Window/Door replacement	54	888	45
Heating system	36	811	61
Roof work	26	433	30
Interior modernization	12	430	–
Flooring	5	65	8
Landscaping	2	24	–
Lighting	1	19	–
Other	19	448	24
Total[a]	155	3118	168

Source: Interview data, CMHC Senior Partnership consultant, April 2012
[a]Totals in this table are not net totals due to overlap of projects or units undertaking several types of retrofit work.

went to nine coops in Edmonton and five coops in Calgary.[9] The retrofits focused on window and door replacement, followed by upgrades to the heating system and roofs (see Table 5.9). These were capital intensive measures, and given the rent revenue constraints in the social housing sector, it was not surprising that providers selected to finance these with grant funds (CHF 2010).

Heating system upgrades constituted a shared retrofit category for cooperatives and non-profits that undertook roof, window replacement, or interior modernization. However, some projects exclusively undertook interior modernizations (e.g. renovating kitchen cabinets and countertops). In general, energy audits were not performed and/or required. For some cooperatives without a strong management capacity, participation in the program was not straight forward as it required a great deal of volunteer time to comply with program guidelines and requirements. CMHC staff in the Prairie Office worked extensively with non-profit and coop organisations to assist with project submissions, alignment of priorities and to increase the success rate of applicants in the second year of the CEAP program (Interview data, Senior Program manager, April 2012). For small cooperatives, the planning, application and approval process took over 2 years while the actual renovation work was performed in a shorter period of time (interview data, Co-ordinator, October 2012).

5.8 Conclusion

The objective of this chapter was to delineate the major categories of retrofit upgrades chosen by different social housing providers, and to evaluate the impact of the CEAP in upgrading the social housing stock in Alberta, particularly in

[9]Information on the total number of co-operatives in Edmonton and Calgary was retrieved from http://www.chfcanada.coop/eng/pages2007/about_3a.asp?Prov=AB.

Edmonton and Calgary. Considerable qualitative upgrades to the housing stock were realised due to the funding administered by the province and CMHC. Undertaking major upgrades was beyond the financial capacity of public, non-profit and cooperative housing providers and would not have materialised or would have been deferred if CEAP grant funding was not available. The retrofit upgrades enhanced the quality of the social housing sector, and in some cases resulted in significant energy savings. Both programs were administered efficiently using existing institutional structures at the central and provincial level, leaving a fair amount of autonomy to the HMBs to decide on the types of retrofits and renovation measures needed.

Despite some diversity, both programs documented that investment in window/door replacement, roofs and heating/mechanical systems was a preferred choice, perhaps due to the capital intensive nature of these measures. In most of the projects, rents were geared to income and there was a limited capacity to fund such improvements through general rent revenue or reserve fund accumulation. The largest HMBs in the province accounted for the largest share of program funds, but took a very different approach to project implementation. CRHC in Edmonton selected several measures and invested across all projects within their portfolio, while CHC in Calgary opted for more comprehensive investment and improvements in selected buildings. Without specific data, it was difficult to say which is better or more strategic, but in both cases energy efficiency was not a priority.

Some of the challenges faced by social housing providers within the retrofit programs related to tight deadlines for program management and administration, which given the sometimes unpredictable nature of construction work led to program extensions and reallocation of funds for other types of measures. The reason behind the unofficial prolongation of the 2-year period of the program was mainly due to the time needed for tendering and contracting retrofit work, as the delays result from permit applications and building inspection processes (Interview data, Program supervisor, August 2012). Some of the smaller HMBs reportedly faced capacity constraints and difficulties in the management of construction work, contracts, and even qualifying for program funds due to complex guidelines and procedures.

References

Alberta Energy Efficiency Alliance. (2010). *Alberta Energy Efficiency Act – Discussion Paper*. Retrieved November 2012 from: http://www.aeea.ca/pdf/EE%20Act%20Discussion%20Paper%20-%20AEEA%20-%20Final%20-%20Jan%202010.pdf

Alberta Government. (2011). *Budget 2011*. Retrieved May 2012 from: http://alberta.ca/acn/201102/2995902%20BudgetSummarybyMinistry_Budget2011%20-%20Final.pdf

Alberta Urban Municipalities Association [AUMA]. (2012). Retrieved November 2012 from:http://www.auma.ca/live/MuniLink/Communications/Member+Notices?contentId=15244

Canada Mortgage and Housing Corporation [CMHC]. (2009). News Releases – June 25. *Canada-Alberta Agreement Boost Affordable Housing Funding*. Retrieved July 2011 from: http://www.cmhc.ca/en/corp/nero/nere/2009/2009-06-25-1230.cfm

Canada Mortgage and Housing Corporation [CMHC]. (2010). *Application guidelines: Renovation and retrofit of existing social housing administered by CMHC*. Ottawa: CMHC.

Canada Mortgage and Housing Corporation [CMHC]. (2011). *Canadian housing observer 2011*. Ottawa: CMHC.

Canada Mortgage and Housing Corporation [CMHC]. (2012). *Success stories*. Ottawa: CMHC. Retrieved October 2012 from:http://www.cmhc.ca/en/inpr/afhoce/sust/sust_114.cfm.

Capital Region Housing Corporation [CRHC]. (2012). CEAP Renovation and retrofit. Retrieved May 2012 from:http://www.crhc.ab.ca/project-development/ceap-renovation-and-retrofit.aspx

City of Calgary. (2011). *2011 Survey of non-market rental housing in Calgary*. Revised September 18, 2012. Retrieved November 2012 from: http://www.calgary.ca/CSPS/CNS/Pages/Social-research-policy-and-resources/2011-Survey-of-Non-Market-Rental-Housing-in-Calgary.aspx

Co-operative Housing Federation of Canada [CHF]. (Fall 2010). *News Brief*. National Edition, 18 (2). Retrieved July 2012 fromhttp://www.chfcanada.coop/eng/pdf/NB/NB2010-11.pdf

Ministry of Housing and Urban Affairs [MHUA]. (2011). *Annual report 2010-2011*. Edmonton: MHUA. Retrieved May 2012 from:http://housing.alberta.ca/documents/2010_11_HUA_annualreport.pdf.

Office of the Auditor General of Ontario. (2009). *Annual Report 2009*. Retrived May 2012 from http://www.auditor.on.ca/en/reports_en/en09/312en09.pdf

Weia, T., & Liu, Y. (2017). Estimation of global rebound effect caused by energy efficiency improvement. *Energy Economics, 66*, 27–34.

Chapter 6
Policy Design of New Energy Efficiency Retrofit Programs in Canada

6.1 Introduction: New Emphasis on Climate Change Imperatives

This chapter provides an overview of the energy efficiency retrofit programs in the social housing sector of three provinces (Ontario, British Columbia and Alberta) in the post *Canada Economic Action Plan* period (2014–2018). It illustrates how different provincial priorities and housing policies affect program design and strategies for implementation. At the national level, as a signatory of the *United Nations Framework Convention on Climate Change*, Canada has set the target of lowering 30% of Canada's GHG emissions compared to the 2005 level by 2030 (Government of Canada 2018a). In 2016, Canada produced 704 megatonnes of carbon dioxide equivalent, out of which 81.4 megatonnes were from the buildings sector (approximately 12%) (Government of Canada 2018b). As such, efforts to curb GHG emission from existing and new buildings will continue to play an important part in achieving the national goal of environmental sustainability. Regulatory efforts include the enforcement of *Energy Efficiency Act 2012* to mandate the use of energy-efficient products in construction and a new *National Energy Building Code* 2017 to raise the technical standards and requirements for energy-efficient design (National Resources Canada 2019; International Energy Agency 2010).

The first *National Housing Strategy* launched in 2017 commits $55 billion over 10 years. The National Housing Co-Investment Fund addresses one of the priorities by providing long term, low-interest loans for the construction and revitalization of affordable housing. The focus of this fund is to develop energy efficient, accessible and socially inclusive housing. The implementation process has been limited, particularly as far as investment in existing social housing is concerned.

The chapter analyzes provincial programs in the social housing sector with a focus on implementation in Vancouver and Toronto to provide state-of-the-art assessment of policy design, funding and institutional structure. The methodology builds on literature review, content analysis of policy documents and interviews with

S. Tsenkova, *Energy Efficient Affordable Housing*,
https://doi.org/10.1007/978-3-030-69563-7_6

program managers. Provincial and territorial jurisdiction over energy efficiency and housing policies as well as the lack of federal energy strategies results in uncoordinated and less systematic programs compared to the *Canada Economic Action Plan* period, which provided $850 million over 2 years for the retrofit of existing social housing (Tsenkova 2013).

6.2 Review of British Columbia Policy and Implementation

To meet Canada's *Paris Agreement* commitments on GHG reduction, $1.4 billion was set aside under the *Low Carbon Economy Leadership Fund* to support initiatives across all provinces and territories. Allocation is according to the population of the respective provinces and territories, so British Columbia received more than $162 million in funding (Government of Canada 2018c). EfficiencyBC is a jointly funded program by the federal and provincial government with each contributing $12 million under the *Low Carbon Economy Leadership Fund* to achieve the province's targeted level of reduced GHG emission (Province of British Columbia 2018). Since 2008, British Columbia has been tracking its carbon footprint and setting out goals to achieve GHG reduction of 80% compared to 2007 level by 2050. Energy efficiency retrofit programs for social housing in Vancouver such as the *Social Housing Retrofit Support Program* (SHRSP), the *EfficiencyBC Social Housing Incentive Program* (BC SHIP) as well as the *Capital Renewal Fund* (CRF) are the province's attempts to accomplish the GHG reduction mandated by law. BC Housing promotes sustainability innovation in social housing retrofits. Programs such as the *Energy Efficiency Retrofit Program* (EERP) have been instrumental in achieving corporate sustainability goals. Energy retrofits in social housing in Vancouver are often joint efforts administered by BC Housing with support from the BC Non-profit Housing Association (BCNPHA) and the main energy service companies BC Hydro and FortisBC. Projects funded by SHRSP, BC SHIP and EERP are of this nature (City of Vancouver 2018).

6.2.1 *Social Housing Retrofit Support Program (SHRSP)*

SHRSP is a joint effort by utility companies, FortisBC and BC Hydro, the province of British Columbia though BC Housing and the Ministry of Energy, Mines and Petroleum Resources (MEMPR) and the BC Non-Profit Housing Association (BCNPHA) representing the non-profit sector. Funded by the utility companies, MEMPR and the federal government, the program is administered by the utility companies (FortisBC n.d.-a, n.d.-b). The program includes: (1) energy study funding for $5,000 provided by FortisBC; (2) up to $7,000 for implementation support—project management, contract administration; and (3) renovation projects that incorporate natural gas and electric energy conservation measures to improve building envelope performance, install energy-efficient equipment or systems and reducing energy consumption for heating and ventilation (efficiencyBC n.d.-a). New equipment installed under this program must be operational for at least 10 years.

Housing societies (non-profit), housing co-operatives and municipal housing providers that are customers of FortisBC or BC Hydro are eligible to apply for SHRSP if the existing residential building has minimum nine units and retrofitted spaces are common areas. The retrofit has to be completed within 12 months and the energy study report has to be submitted within 90 days. Depending on the applicants' needs, the amount of funding varies. In general, rebates depend on the type of energy-conserving products to be installed which range from boilers, insulation, programmable thermostat to lighting, kitchen equipment and electric water heaters (FortisBC n.d.-c). For the energy study funding, applicants must engage an engineering consultant approved by FortisBC who will assist in identifying potential measures that can lead to natural gas and electric energy conservation (ibid). After the energy study is completed, utility companies issue a Capital Approval Incentive Notification setting out the approved list of energy conservation measures, requirements of each measure and their corresponding rebates.

6.2.2 *Efficiency BC Social Housing Incentive Program (SHIP)*

BC SHIP was created to complement SHRSP; it is funded by the federal and provincial governments (efficiencyBC 2018). It offers funding for energy studies, implementation support and retrofit incentives targeting GHG reduction for housing providers with agreements with BC Housing (efficiencyBC n.d.-b). Retrofit types include natural gas and fuel switching measures in existing buildings with documented GHC reductions. Each project that receives funding from BC SHIP is expected to reduce its GHG emission by at least 500 tonnes of CO_2 equivalent in the lifetime of newly installed products or 500 GJs of natural gas per year (ibid). BC Housing Management Commission requires buildings to undergo ASHRAE level 1 audit to ascertain the predicted GHG savings and uses this metric to decide on funding (ibid). Every tonne of CO_2 equivalent reduced leads to an incentive of $70 to a maximum of 75% of project's incremental cost, not exceeding $200,000. Each housing provider is eligible for a maximum of $200,000 in retrofit incentives across their portfolio.

In the first 2 years, the program received $2-million from BC Housing. MEMPR oversees the program administered by BC Housing with the support of BCNPHA. The funding mechanism for retrofit incentives requires a post-implementation review to verify the GHG savings 1 year after the retrofit completion and register the projects on a federal government's software for benchmarking purposes (see Table 6.1 for comparative description).

Table 6.1 Energy efficiency retrofit programs for affordable housing in British Columbia

Eligibility requirements	SHRSP	BC SHIP	EERP	CRF
Building size	More than 9 units	Buildings not eligible under SHRSP	Nil	Nil
Recipients	Non-profit, co-op housing providers City of Vancouver	Non-profit, co-op housing providers City of Vancouver	Non-profit, co-op housing providers City of Vancouver	Non-profit, co-op housing providers City of Vancouver
Scope	Gas and electricity energy conservation measures Optional: Energy study and implementation support	Natural gas efficiency and fuel switching measures Technologies must be widely adopted and not currently covered by SHRSP	Small-scale Take advantage of incentives under utility companies	Major repairs
Timeline		2018	2011	Long term
Other requirements	New equipment installed under this program must be operational for at least 10 years	Retrofits must reduce GHG emission by at least 500 tonnes of CO_2 equivalent in installed products' lifetime GHG savings must be monitored a year following retrofit		

Source: Author's research

6.2.3 Energy Efficiency Retrofit Program (EERP)

EERP was initiated by BC Housing, BCNPHA and BC Hydro in 2011 with FortisBC joining the partnership in 2014. It provides additional funding for eligible social housing providers to take advantage of the existing utility upgrading incentives currently provided by BC Hydro and FortisBC (BC Housing 2015). The type of retrofit intended for EERP is small-scale and short-term with portion of the payoff to be retained by housing providers (BC Housing 2018a). EERP's main goals is to enable non-profit housing providers to improve the energy efficiency of their affordable housing stock and reduce GHG emissions. Since 2001, 284 projects were completed with an estimated energy savings of 6.8 GWh. In 2017, 23 electric and 17 gas-focused energy retrofit projects were funded by EERP that promised a total savings of 409,000 kWh and 6,200 GJ respectively (BC Housing 2018c). Another seven projects received funding in 2018/19 with an estimated energy savings of 0.4 GWh; nine projects were supported in 2019/20 that will yield approximately 0.7 GWh energy savings.

Non-profit, co-operative and municipal housing providers that own or lease social housing developments receiving subsidies under operating agreement with BC Housing are eligible for grants or rebates under the program (BC Housing 2015). Since the program's inauguration, BC Housing has dedicated $2.8 million with $700,000 for 2018/19. BC Housing and BCNPHA administer EERP funding under Hydro's Power Smart Express or Fortis BC's gas-specific program (BC Non-Profit Housing Association 2016).

6.2.4 *Capital Renewal Fund*

British Columbia has committed $1.1 billion to CRF to improve social housing over the next decade with $400 million dedicated to improve its energy performance (Province of British Columbia 2018a). The investment is an integral part of *Homes for BC* affordability plan (Province of British Columbia 2018b). Eligible buildings are owned or leased by non-profit and co-operative housing providers under existing operating agreement with BC Housing. Retrofits are major renovations with seismic and fire-safety upgrades, critical building repairs and measures to reduce GHG emission. Prioritization is done in accordance with the Facility Condition Index (FCI) which measures the cost of needed repairs divided by the building's replacement cost (BC Housing 2018b). BC Housing has committed more funding for CRF with the amount dedicated to the non-profit sector increasing steadily from $55 million in 2018/2019 to approximately $100 million in 2020/21 (Table 6.2). Out of the annual CRF budget, renovation targeted at energy efficiency accounts for $10 million. CRF is expected to bring clean energy technologies to approximately 51,000 social housing units and 7,700 jobs (Province of British Columbia 2018c).

6.3 Review of Policy and Implementation in Ontario

Policies and programs to retrofit affordable housing for energy efficiency in Ontario are responses to the province's efforts to combat climate change and to improve affordable housing stock. Under *Ontario's Climate Change Action Plan* released in 2015, the strategies to reduce GHG emissions to 80% below 1990 levels by 2050, supported several programs targeting social housing retrofits with funding from the

Table 6.2 Total funding committed under capital renewal fund 2018–2021

Committed CRF	2018/19 ($ millions)	2019/20 ($ millions)	2020/21 ($ millions)
Non-profit sector	55.0	94.4	98.4
PRHC[a]	43.1	43.1	46.9
Total	98.1	134.8	145.3

Source: BC Housing Program Manager, 2019

[a]Provincial social and affordable housing portfolio

Table 6.3 Energy efficiency retrofitting programs for affordable housing: Toronto

Eligibility requirements	SHARP	SHAIP	GreenON	SHIP
Building size	Single elevator-serviced apartment buildings At least 150 units	Single elevator-serviced apartment buildings At least 100 units	Single apartment buildings Less than 100 units	Affordable and social housing buildings
Recipients	TCHC Non-profit & Co-op	TCHC	Non-profit & Co-op	TCHC Non-profit & Co-op
Scope	Only specific energy-efficiency retrofits are eligible	Similar to SHARP plus any retrofits that use low-carbon or carbon-free technologies	Similar to SHAIP	Critical repairs including energy efficiency retrofit
Timeline	2016 to first quarter of 2018	2017 to 2021 Cancelled in 2018	2018 to 2021 Cancelled in 2018	2016-2017
Other requirements		Buildings remain affordable for 10 years after retrofit	Buildings have not received funding under SHARP, SHEEP or SHAIP	Buildings remain affordable for 10 years after retrofit

Source: Author's research

province's carbon market (Government of Ontario 2015). The Ontario's carbon market with its cap-and-trade program had been a leading contributor to the province's mandate to fight climate change. The proceeds from this carbon market were instrumental in funding the Green Investment Fund (GIF), the *Green Ontario Fund Social Housing Program* (GreenON) and the *Social Housing Apartment Improvement Program* (SHAIP). The GIF has committed $92 million to reduce GHG emissions in social housing developments through the *Social Housing Apartment Retrofit Program* (SHARP) targeting high-rise social housing and the *Social Housing Electricity Efficiency Program* (SHEEP) geared towards electrically heated houses and townhouses where tenants pay for hydro costs. The GreenON promises to invest $25 million in retrofits of social housing apartment buildings across the province introducing the latest low-carbon and carbon-free energy technologies (Housing Services Corporation 2018). Lastly, the SHAIP promised $556 million for social housing high-rise apartment buildings over 4 years across Ontario, contingent on the revenue received from the cap-and-trade program.

Furthermore, the federal Affordable Housing Initiative funds the *Social Housing Improvement Program* (SHIP) to support critical repairs in social housing buildings in Ontario (Government of Ontario 2018). The program is broader in scope and does not specifically target energy efficiency. Table 6.3. provides a comparison of different programs in the social housing sector (Canada Mortgage and Housing Corporation 2018).

6.3.1 Social Housing Apartment Retrofit Program (SHARP)

The program had a total one-time funding of $82 million across Ontario, which enables social housing providers to carry out retrofit projects of high-rise apartment buildings with more than 150 units to improve energy efficiency and reduce carbon footprint (City of Toronto 2016a, b). SHARP supports the retrofit of twenty three buildings across Ontario, the reduction of GHG emissions by 3600 tonnes over a 20-year period while creating approximately 1,650 jobs (Ministry of Municipal Affairs and Housing 2016).

Toronto's capital allocation of SHARP funding is $43 million (ibid). The city was determined to utilize the funding not only to improve energy efficiency but also to address the much-needed capital repairs in the ageing social housing. Under SHARP's requirements, energy assessment is required to determine projects with greatest impacts and post-project evaluation needs to be in place. Retrofits eligible for funding under SHARP must lead to reduction in GHG emissions, increase in energy efficiency and must be one of these types: installation of energy-efficient building heating and/or cooling equipment; windows and/or exterior doors; lighting systems or insulation of outer and/or inner walls (ibid).

Ontario's social housing service managers submitted their expressions of interests for SHARP funding to the province in February 2016. The City of Toronto requested $126 million after conducting preliminary survey among all eligible housing providers for their retrofit costs (City of Toronto 2016a, b). The *Shelter, Support and Housing Administration* (SSHA) decided on projects to be financed (Ministry of Municipal Affairs and Housing 2016). SSHA contracted ASHRAE level 3 energy audits to examine in detail potential energy savings, costs and performance expectations of capital intensive retrofits to finalise the list of projects based on potential impacts. Toronto Community Housing Corporation (TCHC) received approximately two-thirds of the funding, while non-profit and co-operative housing providers received the remaining (City of Toronto 2016a, b). SSHA entered into Funding Agreements with the housing providers and monitors disbursement of funds, post-project measurement and verification.

6.3.2 Social Housing Apartment Improvement Program (SHAIP)

Announced in August 2017, SHAIP is a 4-year program that enables retrofit of social housing apartment buildings with proceeds from the provincial carbon market

(Ministry of Housing 2017). Eligible projects must be high-rise elevator-serviced social housing apartment buildings with at least 150 units for 2017-2018 funding cycle and at least 100 units for subsequent years' funding (ibid). Housing projects that receive SHAIP funding must remain affordable for a period of 10 years following the retrofit works, including a minimum of 5 years of operating according to the *Housing Services Act,* 2011 (ibid). Eligible types of retrofits are similar to those under SHARP.

The main objectives of SHAIP include reduction of GHG emissions, improvement of living standards of low-income and vulnerable population, reduction of operation costs for social housing providers and creation of local jobs across Ontario (Ministry of Housing 2017). Depending on proceeds from the carbon market, SHAIP was expected to have a total funding of $556 million from 2017 to 2021 (ibid). The City of Toronto was granted a conditional sum of $300 million (City of Toronto 2018a, b). However, due to the cancellation of Ontario's cap-and-trade program in July 2018, the city only received the 2017–2018 funding of $135 million (Ministry of the Environment, Conservation and Parks 2018).

The City of Toronto planned to allocate the first 2 years' funding for TCHC retrofit projects before exploring the opportunities within the non-profits and co-operatives. This is the largest social housing provider in Toronto with the immediate need and capacity to achieve the goals of SHAIP. Due to the cancellation of the program in 2018, TCHC is the only housing provider that utilized funding under SHAIP. On the institutional side, the City of Toronto entered into a Transfer Payment Agreement with the Ministry. SSHA was responsible for administering and allocating funding for retrofits under an agreement with TCHC regarding building condition assessment and monitoring, energy audit, funding disbursement and evaluation requirements. SSHA also coordinated with TCHC to determine the priority among eligible projects for the first 2 years of SHAIP to address the state-of-repair backlogs in TCHC's portfolio and deliver the necessary GHG reduction.

6.3.3 *GreenON Social Housing Program*

This $25-million program was launched in February 2018 as a component of the *Green Ontario Fund* to support energy efficiency retrofits in social housing apartment buildings with less than 100 units (Housing Services Corporation 2018). *GreenON* addresses the gap in eligibility under SHARP and SHAIP by targeting smaller social housing developments. Eligible buildings must not have received funding under other GHG reduction programs. The scope of eligible retrofits for *GreenON* is similar to that of SHAIP and all projects are expected to be completed by March 2021 (Housing Services Corporation n.d.).

Under *GreenON*'s funding, the City of Toronto was allocated a one-time grant of $2.4 million from 2018 to 2021 (City of Toronto 2018a, b). Similar to SHAIP, *GreenON* was cancelled following the removal of the province's cap-and-trade program. The Housing Services Corporation (HSC) was engaged by the not-for-profit *Green Ontario Fund* as the administrator of *GreenON*, providing support to service managers during application and implementation process and tracking projects' progress (Housing Services Corporation 2018). Service managers were required to submit their business cases to HSC, detailing their funding needs, proposed retrofits, timeline and implementation plan. In the case of Toronto, SSHA was acting on behalf of the service managers and entered into agreements with social housing providers and private organizations regarding energy audits and subsequently Funding Agreements with selected housing providers (ibid). SSHA would select retrofit projects based on the urgency of repair works and compliance of the program requirements.

6.3.4 *Social Housing Improvement Program (SHIP)*

As a component of the *Social Infrastructure Fund*, SHIP aims to improve and preserve the quality of social housing with a total commitment of $209 million in 2016-17 through critical and major building repairs (Ministry of Housing 2019). Eligible retrofit includes energy efficiency and water conservation works in addition to major building repairs such as demolition and reconstruction of major building components. The federal government requires that funding be committed by March 2017 and funded projects completed within 2 years of commitment dates. Funded projects have to remain affordable for 10 years after project completion, including a minimum of 5 years of operating according to the *Housing Services Act, 2011* (ibid).

The City of Toronto was allocated a funding of $76 million under SHIP based on its share of social housing units in Ontario (City of Toronto 2017). Until March 2017, the City of Toronto had allocated $72 million of funding under SHIP to housing providers. TCHC received $48 million while other non-profit and co-operative housing providers received $24 million, corresponding to their respective share of units within SSHA's portfolio. The operational aspects of the program are similar. SSHA entered into an administrative agreement with the then Ministry of Housing to receive SHIP funding. It oversees the delivery of the program, including entering into agreements with housing providers and private organizations (City of Toronto 2016a, b) (Table 6.4).

Table 6.4 Funding allocation for energy efficiency retrofitting programs in Toronto

	SHARP	SHAIP	SHIP
TCHC	9 projects $28 million	12 projects $133 million	21 projects $48 million
Non-profits and cooperatives	17 projects $14 million	Nil	66 projects $24 million
Total funding (Toronto)	$42 million	$133 million	$72 million

Source: Author's estimates based on interview data

6.4 Policy for Affordable Housing Retrofits in Alberta

Energy efficiency retrofit policies are aligned with *Alberta's Climate Leadership Plan* to reduce GHG emissions, diversify the economy and create jobs. They are also an integral part of *Alberta's Affordable Housing Strategy*. It aims at maintaining and improving the conditions of existing affordable housing stock as well as increasing its financial and environmental sustainability (Government of Alberta 2017). Alberta's housing policies also contribute to the *National Housing Strategy's* goal of repairing 300,000 existing housing units and the province has signed an agreement to partner with the federal government for its implementation (Government of Canada 2017).

The provincial government launched the *Affordable Housing Energy Savings Program* (AHESP) with a budget of $25 million to increase the environmental and financial sustainability of publicly owned affordable housing province (Government of Alberta 2018). This funding also includes $9 million from the federal government through the *Low Carbon Economy Fund (LCEF)*. As a response to international commitments, LCEF was set up by the government of Canada to provide capital support over a 5-year period starting in 2017 to increase energy efficiency in buildings to reduce GHG emissions across multiple industries (Government of Canada 2019; Natural Resources Canada, 2018).

AHESP's overall objective is to improve energy efficiency and reduce energy consumption of provincially and municipally owned affordable housing. Financial sustainability is achieved through lowered utility cost for low-income households and housing providers. Targeted reduction in GHG emission and energy consumption are 16,000 tonnes and 225,000 GJ per year respectively (Government of Alberta 2018). There are two phases of AHESP with the first focusing on carrying out energy audits at high-priority affordable housing projects and the second initiated in late 2018 targeting implementation of the audit recommendations.

The Alberta Ministry of Seniors and Housing is responsible for coordinating AHESP, reviewing applications from housing providers and allocating funding for eligible projects. The Ministry is also in charge of procuring contractors for energy audits and subsequent retrofits, managing and executing these contracts as well as evaluating and monitoring progress and results of retrofit projects (Government of Alberta 2018). Housing providers are required to assist in the execution of the projects by providing onsite management and scheduling of retrofits. Lastly, they also need to update the Ministry on the progress of energy audits and/or retrofits funded by AHESP and to ensure minimum disruption to tenants.

The program had a limited implementation due to a change in political leadership in the provincial government. Some of the largest affordable housing providers have carried out energy audits in Calgary and Edmonton supported through the first phase of AHESP. While such assessments prioritized funding for projects with highest potential of GHG reduction and energy conservation in some of the oldest affordable housing projects with the highest number of units, the implementation is on hold until funding from senior governments becomes available (CHAC 2019). The

Government of Alberta has undertaken a review of its affordable housing programs in 2020 with the goal of aligning fiscal, financial and regulatory supports and maximizing opportunities for Albertans.

6.5 Conclusion

The overview of the energy efficiency retrofit programs in the social housing sector of three provinces (Ontario, British Columbia and Alberta) in the post *Canada Economic Action Plan* period (2014-2020) illustrates how different provincial priorities and housing policies affect program design and strategies for implementation. At the national level, commitments to climate change have shifted priorities towards GHG emission from existing buildings as an important part in achieving environmental sustainability (Government of Canada 2016). As most of the existing social housing was built in the 1960s and 1970s without much attention to energy-efficient technologies, most of these buildings likely contribute disproportionately to the overall GHG emission of the building sector compared to their relatively smaller share (Van Dyk 1995; Watson et al. 1996). Therefore, policies and funding programs that aid the retrofit of aging social housing stock are necessary, but very much dependent on federal and provincial grants. Such investments address not only environmental priorities, but also social and public health concerns associated with stigmatization and social disadvantage associated with living in social housing (McCormick et al. 2012; Wellesley Institute 2010). As such, upgrading social housing for energy efficiency not only improves places of residence and reduces energy cost but also boost tenants' self-esteem by allowing them to contribute a great part in Canada's mission to lower our carbon footprint for a better and greener future.

The review of programs illustrates the importance of partnerships through public, private and non-profit collaboration in cities as a strategy for implementation. Notwithstanding the complexities of these collaborations, they provide critical opportunities to improve the social housing sector through coordinated investment in different types of retrofits aligning them with program requirements and metrics of performance. Institutional partnerships capitalise on the effective role of the public sector in the mobilization of resources, the efficiencies of private agencies in the development process (design, build) and the hybridity of the non-profit institutions (management, service delivery). The implementation structures (centralised in British Columbia/Alberta and decentralised in Ontario) capitalise on institutional arrangements and practices established during the CEAP phase. The program outreach is more inclusive with deliberate attempts to include the non-profits and cooperative providers in a substantial way. Research findings indicate that in the capital-intensive programs, the non-profit sector received one third (Toronto) to half of the funding (Vancouver). Institutional arrangements and energy audits complemented substantial efforts to build its capacity to manage and execute retrofit and renovation projects.

Programs in Toronto and Vancouver, although smaller in scope, indicate a good commitment to a more systematic approach to energy efficiency retrofits. In the new wave of investment, energy audits are a standard program requirement and program design incentivizes providers to minimize GHG emissions. BC Housing capital program provides specific incentives for performance targets achieved, encouraging environmental sustainability. Vancouver continues its successful collaboration with utility companies to deliver energy conservation projects and to realize British Columbia's GHG reduction goals. The energy efficiency retrofitting programs leverage the utility companies' incentives and their expertise to ensure efficient and effective implementation of retrofits. This public-private partnership adds to the financial sustainability of Vancouver's small-scale retrofits that employ currently available technologies.

Partnerships need strong leadership, often from a city-based housing agency that has the ability to coordinate finance, manage projects in a dynamic real estate environment and deliver on time and budget. Research findings indicate that the implementation process relies on senior government funding (federal and provincial) for capital costs, but more importantly on predictable and stable source of funding (Tsenkova and Youseff 2011). Changes in provincial governments in Ontario and Alberta resulted in cancellation of programs with a negative impact over the social housing sector. In Ontario, funding from the province's carbon market is a good demonstration of effective use of carbon taxes and financial innovation to support retrofits. However, it is also highly susceptible to changes in the province's political leadership. Following the change of government in 2018 and the cancellation of the cap-and-trade program, many of the programs had their funding reduced or withdrawn altogether.

Finally, an important finding is that the implementation of energy efficiency programs in the social housing sector of Canadian cities is a long-term process that will take decades to address the existing gap. It builds on effective partnerships of different levels of government, robust and sustained financial support, alignment of policies and institutional commitment to increase its outreach and deliver results. Such complexity by design makes statements on 'what works' and 'what does not' challenging. Overall, the second wave of programs has been less successful and systematic, resulting in major set backs in the evolutionary change in the social housing system triggered by the CEAP- supported programs. Despite the strong institutional framework and the improved capacity to plan, manage and implement comprehensive retrofits, particularly in Toronto and Vancouver, even large social housing providers have experienced set backs due to lack of sustainable funding. In Alberta, there is a complete reversal to the status quo. The opportunity for innovation and scaling up of best practices, such as investments in renewable energy components, is also limited and non-existent in the not-for-profit and cooperative sector.

References

BC Housing. (2015). *Energy Efficiency Retrofit Program Funding Guide*. BC Housing.

BC Housing. (2018a). *BC Housing's Sustainability Plan*. BC Housing. Retrieved March 23, 2019, from https://www.bchousing.org/publications/livegreen-Housing-Sustainability-Plan.pdf

BC Housing. (2018b). *2018/2019 - 2020/2021 Service Plan.* BC Housing. Retrieved March 23, 2019, from https://www.bcbudget.gov.bc.ca/2018/sp/pdf/agency/bch.pdf

BC Housing. (2018c). *Livegreen Sustainability Report.* Retrieved from https://www.bchousing.org/publications/livegreen-Sustainability-Report.pdf

BC Non-Profit Housing Association. (2016). *Know your building: Energy audits & building condition assessments.* Retrieved March 3, 2019, from https://bcnpha.ca/wp_bcnpha/wp-content/uploads/2016/11/T23-FINAL-2016_11_Energy_Auditing_Presentation.pdf

Canada Mortagage and Housing Corporation. (2018, August 28). *Seed funding.* Retrieved from https://eppdscrmssa01.blob.core.windows.net/cmhcprodcontainer/sf/project/cmhc/pdfs/content/en/seed-funding-highlight-sheet.pdf

CHAC. (2019, January). *CHAC vision - infographic.* Retrieved from https://static1.squarespace.com/static/57e9508bd482e9f5e2b85fd1/t/5c2cf18fc2241bc8b40dabc4/1546449296394/CHAC-Vision+Infographic_20190101.pdf

City of Toronto. (2016a, July 11). *New federal/provincial affordable and social housing investments from the social infrastructure fund.* Retrieved March 9, 2019, from https://www.toronto.ca/legdocs/mmis/2016/cc/bgrd/backgroundfile-94964.pdf

City of Toronto. (2016b). *Ontario green investment fund benefitting social housing - Social Housing Apartment Retrofit Program (SHARP).* Shelter, Support and Housing Administration. Retrieved March 3, 2019, from https://www.toronto.ca/legdocs/mmis/2016/cd/bgrd/backgroundfile-92865.pdf

City of Toronto. (2017). *Social housing capital investment programs – Projects and funding allocations.* Shelter, Support and Housing Administration. Retrieved March 3, 2019, from https://www.toronto.ca/legdocs/mmis/2017/cd/bgrd/backgroundfile-102505.pdf

City of Toronto. (2018a). *Green Ontario Fund (GreenON) benefitting social housing.* Shelter, support and housing administration. Retrieved March 3, 2019, from https://www.toronto.ca/legdocs/mmis/2018/cd/bgrd/backgroundfile-115728.pdf

City of Toronto. (2018b). *Ontario climate action plan - Social housing apartment improvement program (SHAIP).* Retrieved March 3, 2019, from https://www.toronto.ca/legdocs/mmis/2018/bu/bgrd/backgroundfile-110920.pdf

City of Vancouver. (2018). *Housing Vancouver strategy annual progress report and data book 2018.* Vancouver: City of Vancouver. Retrieved March 24, 2019, from https://vancouver.ca/files/cov/2018-housing-vancouver-annual-progress-report-and-data-book.pdf.

CMHC. (2010). *CHS - Public funds and National Housing Act (Social Housing) 2009.* Ottawa: Canada Mortgage and Housing Corporation.

efficiencyBC. (2018). *Participants guide: EfficiencyBC: Social housing incentive program.* efficiencyBC. Retrieved March 23, 2019, from https://efficiencybc.ca/wp-content/uploads/2018/09/EfficiencyBC-Social-Housing-Incentive-Program-Guide_Final.pdf

efficiencyBC. (n.d.-a). *Social Housing Retrofit Support Program.* Retrieved from https://efficiencybc.ca/incentives/social-housing-retrofit-support-program/

efficiencyBC. (n.d.-b). *EfficiencyBC Social Housing Incentive Program.* Retrieved from efficiencyBC: https://efficiencybc.ca/incentives/provincial-retrofit-incentive-program/

FortisBC. (n.d.-a). *Social Housing Retrofit Support Program for Multi-Unit Residential Buildings - terms and conditions.* Retrieved March 22, 2019, from https://fbcdotcomprod.blob.core.windows.net/libraries/docs/default-source/rebates-and-energy-savings-documents/rebates-for-business/socialhousingretrofitsupportprogram_termsconditions.pdf?sfvrsn=af461e35_2

FortisBC. (n.d.-b). *Social housing retrofit support program.* Retrieved from FortisBC: https://www.fortisbc.com/rebates/business/social-housing-retrofit-support-program

FortisBC. (n.d.-c). *Rebates for social housing retrofit support program.* Retrieved from https://www.fortisbc.com/rebates-and-energy-savings/rebates-and-offers/rebates-business/rebates-for-social-housing-retrofit-support-program

Government of Alberta. (2017). *Alberta's Provincial Affordable Housing Strategy Summary.* Ministry of Seniors and Housing. Retrieved from https://open.alberta.ca/dataset/18c109bc-e567-4f61-b9e4-8973b0b246c4/resource/66dafa3a-c307-441a-8dd8-5c7aac66d025/download/pahssummary.pdf

Government of Alberta. (2018). *Program guide to affordable housing energy savings program*. Edmonton: Ministry of Seniors and Housing.

Government of Canada. (2016). *Energy efficiency regulations*. Retrieved from https://www.canada.ca/en/natural-resources-canada/news/2016/04/energy-efficiency-regulations.html

Government of Canada. (2017). *Canada's national housing strategy*. Retrieved from https://www.placetocallhome.ca/pdfs/Canada-National-Housing-Strategy.pdf

Government of Canada. (2018a). *Canadian Environmental - Sustainability Indicators Greenhouse gas emissions*. Gatineau: Ministry of Environment and Climate Change. Retrieved March 19, 2019, from https://www.canada.ca/content/dam/eccc/documents/pdf/cesindicators/greenhouse-gas-emissions/greenhouse-gas-emissions-en.pdf.

Government of Canada. (2018b). *Greenhouse gas emissions*. Retrieved from https://www.canada.ca/en/environment-climate-change/services/environmental-indicators/greenhouse-gas-emissions.html

Government of Canada. (2018c, July 9). *Low Carbon Economy Fund: Allocations to Provinces and Territories under the Low Carbon Economy Leadership Fund*. Retrieved from Government of Canada: https://www.canada.ca/en/environment-climate-change/news/2017/06/low_carbon_economyfundallocationstoprovincesandterritoriesundert.html

Government of Canada. (2019, April 18). *The low carbon economy fund*. Retrieved from https://www.canada.ca/en/environment-climate-change/services/climate-change/low-carbon-economy-fund.html

Government of Ontario. (2015). *Ontario's climate change strategy*. Retrieved March 1, 2019, from https://docs.ontario.ca/documents/4928/climate-change-strategy-en.pdf

Government of Ontario. (2018, February). *Investment in affordable housing*. Retrieved March 3, 2019, from Ministry of Municipal affairs and housing: http://www.mah.gov.on.ca/Page17675.aspx

Housing Services Corporation. (2018). *GreenON social housing program - Program guidelines*. Retrieved March 1, 2019, from https://www.hscorp.ca/wp-content/uploads/2018/02/One-Pager-GreenON-Final.pdf

Housing Services Corporation. (n.d.). *GreenON Social Housing*. Retrieved March 3, 2019, from https://www.hscorp.ca/wp-content/uploads/2018/02/One-Pager-GreenON-Final.pdf

International Energy Agency. (2010). *Energy policies of IEA Countries - Canada 2009 review*. Paris: International Energy Agency.

McCormick, N. J., Joseph, M. L., & Chaskin, R. J. (2012). The new stigma of relocated public housing residents: Challenges to social identity in mixed-income developments. *City & Community, 11*(3), 285–308.

Ministry of Housing. (2017). *Social Housing Apartment Improvement Program (SHAIP) - Program Guidelines*. Queen's Printer for Ontario.

Ministry of Housing. (2019). *Overview of the 2016 Social Infrastructure Fund (SIF)*.

Ministry of Municipal Affairs and Housing. (2016, February 12). *Ontario Investing $92 Million to Create Jobs and Retrofit Social Housing*. Retrieved March 3, 2019, from Government of Ontario: https://news.ontario.ca/mma/en/2016/02/ontario-investing-92-million-to-create-jobs-and-retrofit-social-housing.html

Ministry of the Environment, Conservation and Parks. (2018). *Ontario Introduces Legislation to End Cap and Trade Carbon Tax Era in Ontario*. Retrieved March 9, 2019, from Government of Ontario: https://news.ontario.ca/ene/en/2018/07/ontario-introduces-legislation-to-end-cap-and-trade-carbon-tax-era-in-ontario.html

National Resources Canada. (2019). *National Energy Code of Canada for Buildings 2017*. Retrieved from https://nrc.canada.ca/en/certifications-evaluations-standards/codes-canada/codes-canada-publications/national-energy-code-canada-buildings-2017

Natural Resources Canada. (2018). *EnerGuide-rated new homes*. Retrieved from https://www.nrcan.gc.ca/energy/efficiency/homes/20578

Province of British Columbia. (2018, September 28). *New program makes saving energy more affordable*. Retrieved from Energy, Mines and Petroleum Resources: https://news.gov.bc.ca/releases/2018EMPR0052-001891

Province of British Columbia. (2018a). *CleanBC*. Retrieved March 23, 2019, from https://blog.gov.bc.ca/app/uploads/sites/436/2019/02/CleanBC_Full_Report_Updated_Mar2019.pdf

Province of British Columbia. (2018b). *Homes for B.C.* Retrieved March 22, 2019, from https://www.bcbudget.gov.bc.ca/2018/homesbc/2018_homes_for_bc.pdf

Province of British Columbia. (2018c, November 22). *B.C. to improve social housing, while reducing pollution*. Retrieved from BC Gov News: https://news.gov.bc.ca/releases/2018PREM0084-002249

Tsenkova, S. (2013). *Retrofits for the future: Affordable housing and energy efficiency programs in Canada*. Calgary: University of Calgary. Retrieved February 10, 2019, from https://ucalgary.ca/cities/files/cities/EnergyRetrofitsTsenkova2013.pdf.

Tsenkova, S., & Youssef, K. (2011). Green and Affordable Housing in Canada: Investment Strategies of Social Housing Organisations. *ENHR Conference 2011*. Toulouse. Retrieved March 18, 2019, from https://www.enhr.net/documents/2011%20France/WS11/Paper-SashaTsenkova-W11.pdf

Van Dyk, N. (1995). Financing social housing in Canada, housing policy debate. *Housing Policy Debate, 6*(4), 815–848.

Watson, R. T., Zinyowera, M. C., & Moss, R. H. (1996). *Climate change 1995 impacts, adaptations and mitigation of climate change: Scientific-technical analyses*. Cambridge: Cambridge University Press. Retrieved March 19, 2019, from http://www.repositorio.cenpat-conicet.gob.ar/bitstream/handle/123456789/577/climateChange1995ImpactsAdpatationsMitigation.pdf?sequence=1.

Wellesley Institute. (2010). *Precarious housing in Canada*. Toronto: Wellesley Institute Report.

Chapter 7
New Energy Efficiency Retrofit Programs in Toronto and Vancouver

7.1 Introduction, Objectives and Methodology

This chapter explores the implementation of energy efficiency measures through *Social Housing Apartment Improvement Program* (SHAIP) and the *Social Housing Apartment Retrofit Program* (SHARP) in Toronto. The research profiles one of the projects in Vancouver funded through the *Capital Renewal Fund* (CRF), which supports social housing retrofits by public and non-profit providers with existing agreements with BC Housing. The comparative case study analysis complements the review of the main energy retrofit programs implemented since 2014 in the two cities with a focus on funding mechanisms, implementation criteria and types of retrofits.

Four case studies from Toronto's social housing portfolio were identified to illustrate program implementation and outcomes. The case studies were selected to represent the renovation strategies of major types of social/affordable housing providers in Toronto: (i) Toronto Community Housing Corporation (TCHC); and (ii) non-profit housing corporations. The selection was guided by recommendations from the Managers and the project leads from the City of Toronto's Social Housing Unit. The projects represented comprehensive retrofits funded under SHAIP and SHARP. Similar approach guided the selection of the case study in Vancouver. Each housing provider agreed to participate in the study.

The methodology included literature review, content analysis of major policy documents and case study project information. In addition, comparative data were validated through key informant interviews undertaken in April-September 2019. Emphasis was placed on a systematic comparison of the types of energy efficiency retrofits and renovation measures to highlight different investment strategies and to document simple return on investment. Retrofit measures were grouped in three major categories: (1) major mechanical; (2) non-mechanical/building envelope; and (3) renewable energy.

The research presented detailed comparative analysis of the following projects:

S. Tsenkova, *Energy Efficient Affordable Housing*,
https://doi.org/10.1007/978-3-030-69563-7_7

1. Kennedy Glamorgan high-rise building with 184 apartments, managed by TCHC; retrofits supported through SHAIP with funding of $8,032,855;
2. Jane Falstaff high-rise building with 224 apartments, managed by TCHC; retrofits supported through SHAIP with funding of $12,464,821;
3. City Park Co-operative on Church Street high-rise building with 256 apartments, managed by a housing coop; retrofits supported through SHARP with funding of $1,380,917;
4. City Park Co-operative on Alexander Street high-rise building with 184 apartments, managed by a housing coop; retrofits supported through SHARP with funding of $930,698;
5. Kingston Public Housing high-rise building with 419 apartments, managed by TCHC; retrofits supported through SHARP with funding of $4,147,960;
6. Grandview Terrace has 154 apartments and town houses, managed by BC Housing; retrofits supported through CRF with $700,000.

Detailed project profiles are available in the Annex of the book. Retrofit measures were grouped in three major categories: (1) major mechanical; (2) non-mechanical/building envelope; and (3) other/renewable energy. Data illustrated projected energy savings (electricity and gas), costs for each measure, GHG reduction, costs and simple return on investment. The following section presents highlights on three of the projects implemented in Toronto and Vancouver.

7.2 Case Study Profiles

City Park Cooperative on Church street was built in 1954. The building has a mix of housing units (1–2 bedroom) with near market rents. The development had 254 apartments with a small share of RGI units (Fig. 7.1). The housing coop implemented a one-year retrofit program incorporating mechanical systems and lighting upgrades. A new solar wall installation provided renewable energy. Table 7.1 describes these measures with a reference to costs, GHG reduction and simple return on investment. While the reduction in annual usage of electricity and gas was substantial, the high cost of some retrofits did not make them viable through a cost recovery mechanism (Internat Energy Solutions 2016a, b).

Kingston Street Public Housing was built in 1968. The project had 419 units provided to low-income tenants on rent-geared-to-income basis. Managed and operated by TCHC, it received over $6 million grant funding from SHARP for a complete retrofit with substantial improvements to building envelope, heating and cooling systems and other upgrades. The retrofits resulted in reduced annual energy consumption cost of $200,000 and GHG reduction of 300 tonnes per year. While TCHC was very efficient in its project planning and execution, which led to economies of scale, the high cost of the complete retrofit package was justified by social and environmental considerations. The project was well-aligned with energy

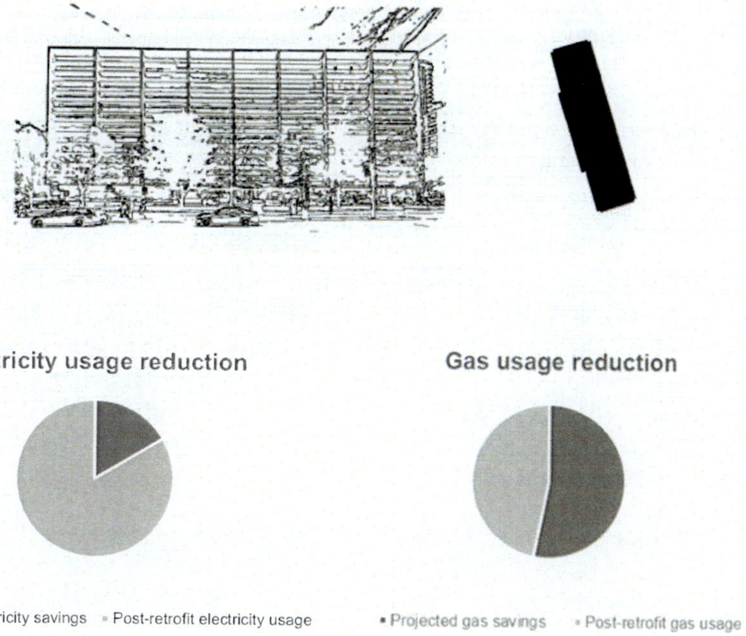

Fig. 7.1 City Park Cooperative Retrofits in Toronto. *Source: Author (top); Author's estimates of annual savings based on energy audit reports (bottom)*

retrofit objectives, but also addressed much-needed quality improvements in the building and provided funding for life cycle replacement of building components. Works were completed on schedule and budget, which at the scale of this development was a substantial accomplishment (Fig. 7.2 and Table 7.2).

Grandview Terrace was a housing development owned and operated by BC Housing. Built in 1967 it consisted of town houses and high-rise apartments providing 154 units to low-income households (Fig. 7.3). This was an example of a more comprehensive retrofit program, planned at the end of the previous CEAP funding cycle, but executed when additional grants became available. The package included mechanical and building envelope measures with a total cost exceeding $700,000. Annual GHG savings were close to 90 tonnes per year and the reduction in energy and gas consumption was about a quarter of pre-retrofit values (see Table 7.3). The simple pay back of substantial upgrades to the building envelope exceeded 100 years, so the decisions to carry out these retrofits were driven by environmental and social factors.

Table 7.1 Costs, energy savings and payback per retrofit type: city park cooperative

Type of retrofit	Projected annual savings				Retrofit cost ($)	Anticipated simple payback[a] (years)
	Projected gas savings (m^3)	Projected electricity savings (kWh)	GHG savings (tonnes)	Cost savings ($)		
Renewable energy						
Solar wall	10,099		19	2,525	53,697	21.3
Mechanical						
Heating and Domestic Hot Water System Upgrade[b]	69,983	44,127	135	28,115	713,432	25.4
Building Automation System Upgrade[c]	2,349	2,598	5	977	65,000	66.5
Non-mechanical						
Lighting Retrofit[d]		117,851	6	17,678	27,858	1.6
Total	82,431	164,576	165	49,295	859,987[e]	

Source: *Energy Audit Reports and Interview data, 2019*
[a]Figures are calculated by dividing the Retrofit Cost by the Annual Cost Savings
[b]Energy Conservation Measures ECM.2 & ECM.3 in Energy Audit Report
[c]Building Renewal Measure BRM.6 in Energy Audit Report
[d]Energy Conservation Measures ECM.4 & ECM.7 in Energy Audit Report
[e]Building Renewal Measure BRM.6 in Energy Audit Report

7.3 Environmental, Economic and Social Outcomes in Case Study Projects

It is noticeable that retrofits in the six case study projects indicate a shift to more comprehensive measures that go beyond retrofits targeting the low-hanging fruits of energy efficiency. The analysis in the section focuses on environmental, economic and social outcomes highlighting diversity of investment strategies. Most of the projects included upgrading of major building components, such as building automation system and makeup air units that are costly, time-consuming and require a high degree of expertise in planning and execution (see Fig. 7.4). These retrofits addressed building components that not only improve energy efficiency performance but also raised residents' living comfort considerably, despite their usually longer payback period. The cost of window replacement was the highest ($9 million), followed by cladding (close to $6 million). The provision of funding from various programs allowed the implementation of capital-intensive retrofits that are not economically viable. The capacity to combine multiple funding sources was stronger for large and capable housing providers such as TCHC as they were the only provider that was able to implement retrofits with payback periods higher than 70 years, such as over-cladding, window and makeup air upgrades.

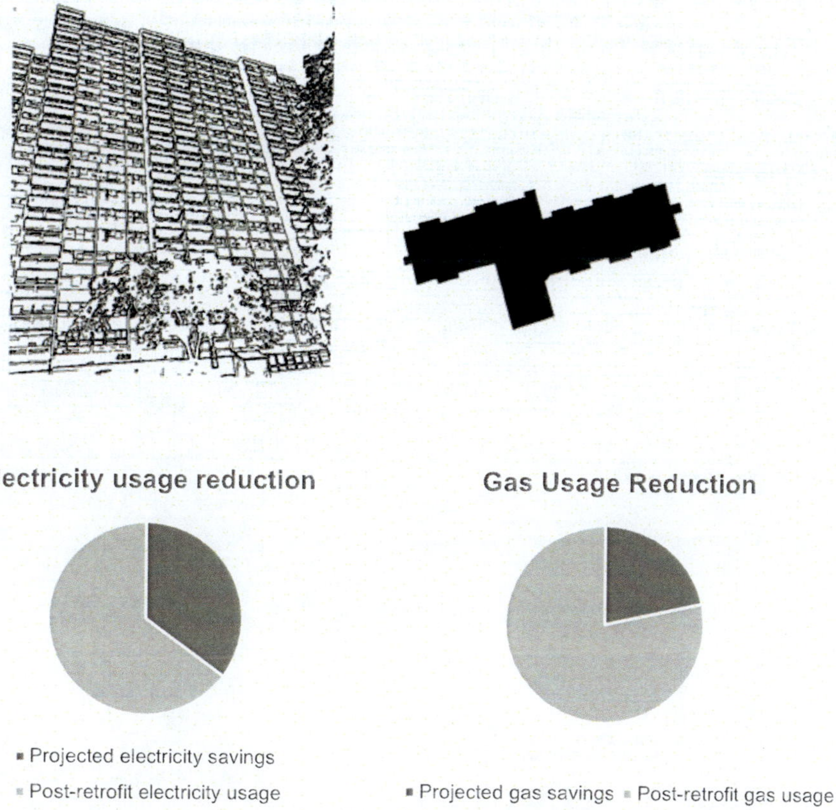

Fig. 7.2 Kinston Street Public Housing Retrofits in Toronto. Source: *Author (top); Author's estimates of annual savings based on energy audit reports (bottom)*

Despite receiving about 85% of Toronto's funding from three social housing programs, TCHC carried out 42 retrofit projects compared to 83 projects for the non-profit and co-op sector. This speaks to the generally worse-off conditions of its portfolio with larger, older apartment buildings with RGI units where the rents do not allow recovery of operational and maintenance costs. The housing provider was much more dependent on cash infusion to address the more extensive nature of energy efficiency retrofits through one-time grants. By comparison, the non-profit sector where rents are set at near market levels had better housing conditions, but lacked system upgrades to makeup air units, heating system updates and better cladding that come with higher price tags and longer payback periods. Compared with Toronto, energy retrofit programs in Vancouver largely targeted small retrofits and very few projects received support from CRF (Prism Engineering 2016).

Table 7.2 Costs, energy savings and payback per retrofit type: Kinston

	Projected annual savings					
Type of retrofit	Projected gas savings (m3)	Projected electricity savings (kWh)	GHG savings (tonnes)	Cost savings	Retrofit cost	Anticipated simple payback[a] (years)
Mechanical						
Heating and Domestic Hot Water System Upgrade	38,338	119,900	82	28,929	1,091,088	37.7
Makeup Air Unit Upgrade	10,185	25,130	21	6,790	472,000	69.5
Building Automation System Upgrade	1,597	4,996	3	1,205	20,000	16.6
Non-mechanical						
Window Retrofit	65,517	204,899	140	49,437	4,860,000	98.3
Lighting Retrofit	–	807,192	64.71	107,514.67	439,151	4.1
Total	115,638	1,162,117	311	193,876	6,882,239	

Source: Energy Audit Reports and Interview data, 2019

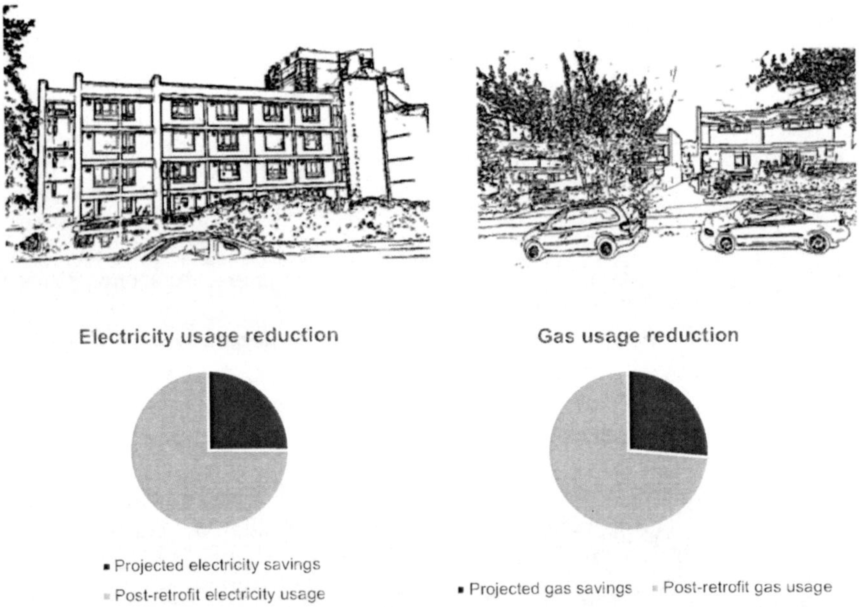

Fig. 7.3 Grandview Terrace Retrofits in Vancouver. Source: *Author (top); Author's estimates of annual savings based on energy audit reports (bottom)*

Table 7.3 Costs, energy savings and payback per retrofit type: Grandview terrace

Type of retrofit	Projected annual savings				Retrofit cost ($)	Anticipated simple payback[b] (years)
	Projected gas savings (m^3)	Projected elect savings (kWh)	GHG savings (tonnes)	Cost Savings ($)		
Mechanical						
Heating and Domestic Hot Water System Upgrade[c]	1,423.21	10,200.00	2.70	1,350	27,700	20.5
Non-mechanical						
Bathroom retrofit[d]	20,300.87		37.70	6,450	24,000	3.7
Window/Door Retrofit[e]	28,383.62		52.70	9,010	175,700	19.5
Lighting Retrofit[f]		26,680.00	0.30	5,560	56,100	10.1
Wall insulation[g]	7,518.84		14.00	2,390	267,500	111.9
Total	50,107.70	36,880.00	93.40	24,760.00[h]		

Source: Energy Audit Reports and Interview data, 2018
[a]Figures are calculated by dividing the Retrofit Cost by the Annual Cost Savings
[b]Figures are calculated by dividing the Retrofit Cost by the Annual Cost Savings
[c]Energy Savings Measures 5.3 & 5.5 in Energy Audit Report
[d]Energy Savings Measure 5.13 in Energy Audit Report
[e]Energy Savings Measure 5.12 and Capital Upgrade 6.4 in Energy Audit Report
[f]Energy Savings Measures 5.1 & 5.2 in Energy Audit Report
[g]Capital Upgrade 6.5 in Energy Audit Report
[h]Inclusive of operation savings

7.3.1 Environmental Outcomes

Buildings are large GHG emitters in Canadian cities and residential buildings often contribute more than half of building emissions. In Toronto, 7.9 megatonnes of GHG are produced by buildings in 2017, 51% from residential buildings (City of Toronto 2019, p. 16). Likewise, buildings in Vancouver account for 41% of the city's total GHG emissions with residential buildings generating 42% of this amount (Metro Vancouver n.d.). As such, energy retrofit projects targeting social housing in these major cities have contributed greatly to the cities' sustainability goals given the energy intensity of most social housing projects (Toronto Community Housing Corporation 2009a, b, c). Annually, the profiled housing projects have led to a reduction in GHG in the range of 100 to 750 tonnes with Falstaff Avenue project having the best performance in this respect. The annual GHG reduction per unit was also high in projects with more comprehensive retrofits (see Fig. 7.5).

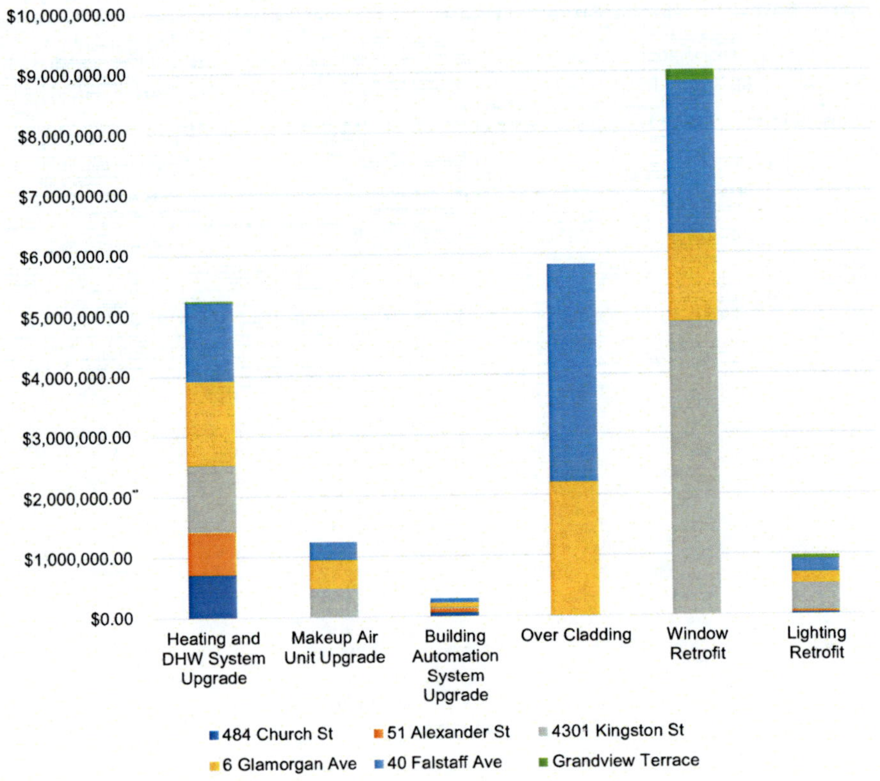

Fig. 7.4 Comparative cost of different type of retrofits. *Source: Author's estimates based on interview data*

7.3.2 Economic and Social Outcomes

The energy savings, when translated to monetary savings, amounted to an annual cut of $25,000 to $226,000 in utility cost. This affects the financial sustainability of the affordable housing project and reduces tenants' expenditure on utility charges (Fig. 7.6).

With the exception of the Kingston Street housing development, the other TCHC projects received a much higher investment per unit which corresponds to the higher investment required to achieve GHG reduction. It is more costly to reduce a tonne of GHG emission per year in TCHC's buildings (PMC Engineering Solutions 2016; PMC Engineering Services 2018). This may be directly linked with the generally poorer conditions of TCHC's portfolio and the fact that most TCHC tenants are socially vulnerable households living in rent-geared-to-income housing. The energy retrofit projects not only improved the comfort of their homes but also inspire community building initiatives and a new sense of pride. Every household living

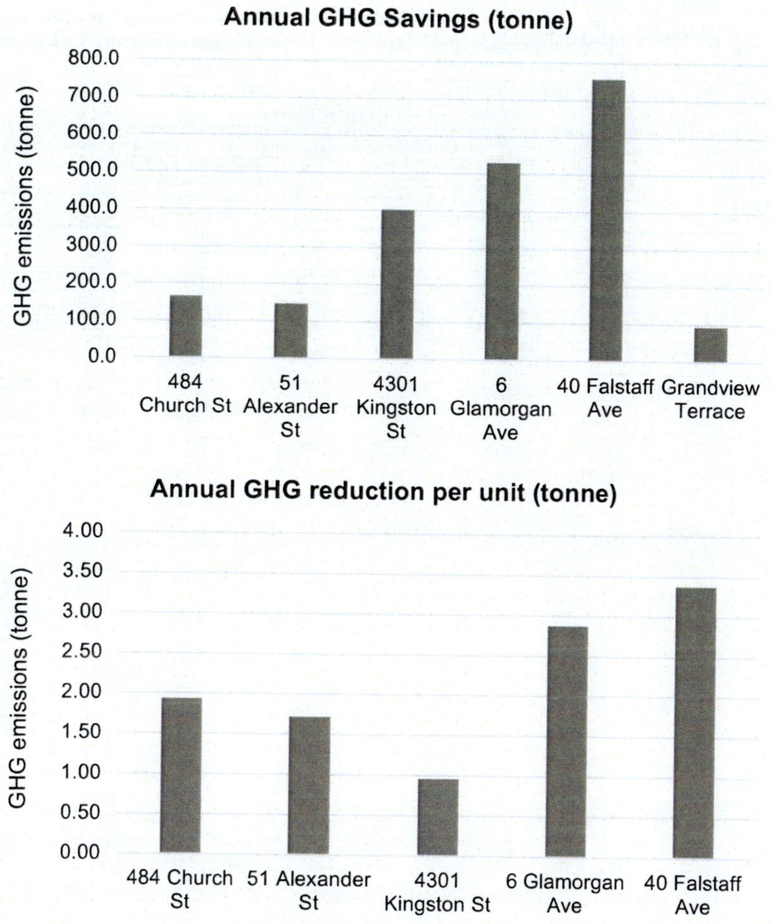

Fig. 7.5 Environmental Performance: GHG Savings. *Source: Author's estimates based on energy audit reports*

in the case study housing projects benefited from retrofit investment in the range of \$10,000 to \$55,600, which was part of the government's effort to reduce GHG emissions but also an indication of commitment to most socially disadvantaged residents (Fig. 7.5). Another indirect achievement of energy retrofit projects was the creation of green jobs. Based on Canadian Centre for Policy Alternative' estimate, the profiled retrofit projects in Toronto alone generated approximately 430 local direct jobs every year, about 50–60 times the number of jobs the same investment in oil and gas would create (Lee and Carlaw 2010).

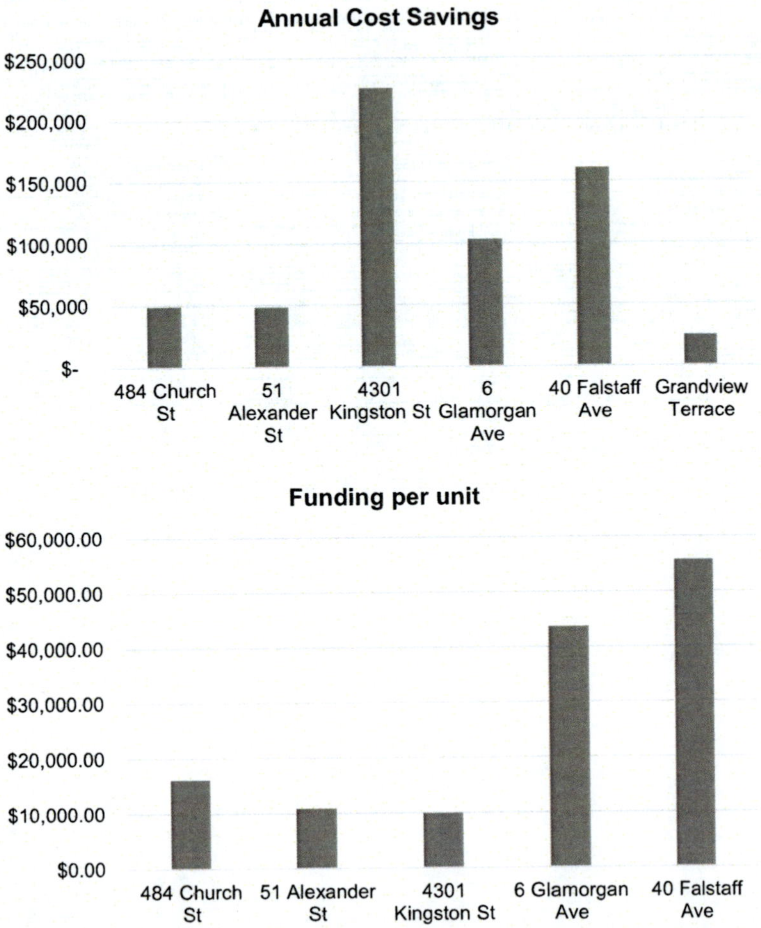

Fig. 7.6 Economic Performance: Cost Savings. *Source: Author's estimates based on energy audit reports*

7.4 Concluding Comments: Opportunities and Challenges

The programs have provided timely and much-needed funding to address the energy-inefficient and deteriorating social housing stock in Toronto and Vancouver. Collectively, the energy retrofit programs in Toronto provided $247 million to various housing providers to carry out capital repairs and system upgrades in social housing. In the process, approximately 13% of TCHC's portfolio and 33% of the non-profit and co-op sectors' benefited. Different programs were complimentary in terms of eligibility, costs and types of retrofits. Although much smaller in scope, the programs in Vancouver allowed for adoption of energy conservation technologies (BC Housing n.d.). Overall, the energy retrofit programs have managed to improve the quality of existing affordable housing projects while reducing their carbon footprint resulting in GHG reduction in the built environment.

7.4.1 *Opportunities*

The institutional frameworks of different programs ensured fair distribution of the limited funding. In Toronto, the City allocated two thirds of its SHARP and SHIP funding to the municipal company and the rest to non-profit and co-op housing providers, which corresponds to their respective share of the city's social housing stock. In Vancouver SHRSP funding was administered by the utility companies, while Efficiency BC reimbursed projects based on their actual GHG reduction. The execution of more comprehensive retrofits ensured economies of scale where the project design, procurement, contract management and execution was coordinated and implemented in a timely manner. TCHC and BC Housing have established relationship with contractors and sound project management systems. The energy efficiency audit requirement was beneficial in packaging types of retrofits with the highest environmental benefits—reduction in energy costs and GHG emissions.

In both cities the institutional structure for program administration capitalised on institutional arrangements set up for the retrofit programs under the previous *Canada Economic Action Plan*. Such continuity made the follow up smaller programs more efficient. An overall attempt to ensure fairness and consistency in program funding allocation was evident with a specific emphasis on the involvement of smaller non-profit and cooperative housing providers. While market penetration of retrofit technologies was small, the institutional frameworks benefited from partnerships with a strong public sector lead. Both approaches have produced successes as Toronto's decentralized method consolidated many critical functions in a key organization for higher efficiency, consistency and more support dedicated to smaller housing providers. Vancouver's strategy utilized the competitive advantages of a centralised administration by BC Housing working in partnership with other sectors to deliver accessible retrofit options.

7.4.2 *Challenges*

With multiple funding opportunities for energy retrofits, each with its own set of criteria and administrative processes to follow, small and less experienced housing providers may have had a hard time accessing these funds. Large providers such as TCHC and BC Housing were more well-versed with the nuances of different programs and were able to combine various sources of funding to finance more extensive retrofits. Non-profit housing providers prioritized energy conservation measures that have shorter payback periods such as lighting over large-ticket items such as cladding or window replacement. Despite the differences in the way these energy retrofit initiatives were set up, the funding sources were not necessarily reliable. Many of the programs discussed were one-off with no commitment for renewal. This has created tremendous difficulty for funding administrators to determine criteria for distribution of limited resources. Some affordable housing projects were in need of funding for critical structural upgrades that may not result in energy efficiency. It was also a balancing act between equity in funding allocation vs effectiveness to insure impactful retrofits.

As the featured retrofit projects suggest, many building components in affordable housing developments were costly and not necessarily viable to retrofit in terms of simple return on investment. Developing new technologies and methodologies will be essential to solve the economic challenge of retrofitting affordable housing for energy efficiency (Heerema 2017). For housing organisations whose operating agreements consider utility cost as "uncontrolled expenses", any cost savings as a result of energy retrofits will lessen the amount of subsidy provinces have to provide (Frappé-Sénéclauze et al. 2017). This adversely affects the post-retrofit cash flow for housing providers as financial savings due to capital-intensive retrofits are registered as reduction in equity rather than reduction in operating expenses, making the pay-back period for such projects even longer.

While carbon pricing and environmental policies are effective in curbing GHG emissions, they do not provide a stable source of funding for energy retrofits in the social housing sector (O'Reilly 2019; Pembina Institute 2018). Ontario's cancellation of their cap-and-trade program illustrates this point. The sector needs a sustainable public sector commitment that recognises the synergy of environmental, economic and social benefits.

References

BC Housing. (n.d.). *Directly Managed Properties*. Retrieved from BC Housing: https://www.bchousing.org/housing-assistance/tenant-programs-resources/directly-managed-properties

Canada Mortgage & Housing Corporation. (2019, May 21). *First Ever Passive House High-Rise Retrofit in Canada Will Create More Affordable Housing for Seniors in Hamilton*. Retrieved from Canada Mortgage & Housing Company: https://www.cmhc-schl.gc.ca/en/media-newsroom/news-releases/2019/first-ever-passive-house-high-rise-retrofit-canada-create-more-affordable-housing-senior-hamilton

City of Toronto. (2019). *Social housing programs*. Toronto: City of Toronto.

Frappé-Sénéclauze, T.-P., Heerema, D., & Bobyn, D. (2017). *Aggregation of energy retrofits in affordable housing: Opportunities and challenges in adapting the Energiesprong model in B.C.* Pembina Institute.

Heerema, D. (2017, July 19). *Better homes, lower costs, less pollution: The Energiesprong model and B.C. buildings*. Retrieved from Pembina Institute: https://www.pembina.org/blog/affordable-housing-renewal

Internat Energy Solutions. (2016a). *Energy Assessment Report: City Park Cooperative 484 Church St., Toronto, Ontario*. Toronto, ON: Internat Energy Solutions Canada Inc.

Internat Energy Solutions. (2016b). *Energy Assessment Report: City Park Cooperative 51 Alexander St., Toronto, Ontario*. Toronto, ON: Internat Energy Solutions Canada Inc.

Lee, M., & Carlaw, K. (2010). *Climate justice, green jobs and sustainable production in BC*. Vancouver, BC: Canadian Center for Policy Alternatives.

O'Reilly, D. (2019, March 29). *Hamilton's Ken Soble Tower rebirth a Passive House first*. Retrieved from Daily Commericial News by ConstructConnect: https://canada.constructconnect.com/dcn/news/projects/2019/03/hamiltons-ken-soble-tower-rebirth-passive-house-first

Pembina Institute. (2018). *Affordable housing renewal: Retrofits at scale - workshop summary*. Pembina Institute.

PMC Engineering Services. (2018). *Energy Audit Report - 40 Falstaff Ave, North York, Ontario*. PMC Engineering Services.

PMC Engineering Solutions. (2016). *Energy Audit Report - 4301 Kingston Road, Scarborough, ON*. Toronto, ON: PMC Engineering Solutions.

PMC Engineering Solutions. (2018). *Energy Audit Report - 6 Glamorgan Ave, Scarborough, ON*. PMC Engineering Solutions.

Prism Engineering. (2016). *Detailed Energy Audit Report - Grandview Terrace 1441 Graveley St, Vancouver*. Burnaby, BC: Prism Engineering.

Toronto Community Housing Corporation. (2009a). *Northeast - Family Housing - 3 Bedroom Units*. Retrieved from https://www.torontohousing.ca/residents/your-tenancy/Documents/NORTHEAST%20FAMILY%203-BED%20UNITS%20MAP%20and%20LIST%202011.pdf

Toronto Community Housing Corporation. (2009b). *Northwest - Family Housing - 1 Bedroom Units*. Retrieved from https://www.torontohousing.ca/residents/your-tenancy/Documents/NORTHWEST%20FAMILY%201-BED%20UNITS%20MAP%20and%20LIST%202011.pdf

Toronto Community Housing Corporation. (2009c). *Northeast - Family Housing - 2 Bedroom Units*. Retrieved from https://www.torontohousing.ca/residents/your-tenancy/Documents/NORTHEAST%20FAMILY%202-BED%20UNITS%20MAP%20and%20LIST%202011.pdf

Chapter 8
Retrofits for the Future: Lessons from Affordable Housing and Energy Efficiency Programs in Canada

8.1 Evolutionary Change in the Social Housing Sector

Recognizing the potential impact of energy savings in housing, the research reviewed the effect of new federal and provincial initiatives on energy efficiency retrofits in the social housing sector. The comparative analysis focused on the experiences of three provinces in Canada—BC, Ontario and Alberta—to highlight the diversity of approaches, program achievements and challenges in program implementation. Highlights from nineteen case studies of best practices in the four largest cities illustrate a range of investment strategies deployed by public, non-profit and cooperative housing providers. The social housing sector was targeted as a field of policy intervention, where socially responsible and very professional housing providers have the potential to capitalize on government funding to leverage further investment in energy efficiency retrofits as well as to showcase the results of emerging transformation. The research points to several interrelated opportunities. First, an energy efficient social housing stock contributes to the larger objective of mitigating climate changes resulting from GHG emissions. Second, in regards to the low-income families and social tenants, an energy efficient social dwelling reduces utility costs and thus shields them from energy poverty. Third, energy efficiency activities have the potential for creating jobs in the local economy with spill over economic effects on local businesses, suppliers and service providers. Finally, energy retrofits and better housing conditions in social housing have a positive impact on the well-being of tenants and thus reduce their dependence on other social services and support (Tsenkova 2013, 2018).

The research documents challenges in the implementation process as well as profiles innovative responses that tend to be efficient in economic and environmental terms. Similar approaches have been used in the European Union and the United States to pilot test the mix of regulatory, fiscal and financial measures designed to promote energy efficiency implementation (Brophy et al. 2010). Such policy reforms recognize the growing importance of energy efficiency retrofits in environmental

S. Tsenkova, *Energy Efficient Affordable Housing*,
https://doi.org/10.1007/978-3-030-69563-7_8

terms, but also the economic and social benefits of green job creation, lower housing costs, improved housing quality, health and community well-being (Stephenson et al. 2010). While the emphasis in this review is on the social housing sector, this first systematic assessment has the potential to offer important insights into policy responses that might benefit the residential sector as a whole. As the number of successful projects grows, green and affordable housing could be seen as a proven, cost-effective approach to creating healthy, vibrant communities. These advances in implementation, due in large part to public sector leadership, could signal an emerging transformation in housing and energy policy through federal and provincial commitment. The engagement of government agencies and social housing institutions is critical for the continued success in the implementation process to capitalize on the evolutionary change in the last decade.

8.2 Success of Energy Efficiency Retrofit Programs (2009–2013)

Canada's Economic Action Plan (CEAP) provided a major opportunity for the implementation of a comprehensive package of retrofits and improvements in the social housing sector. The two programs—managed by the provinces and by the Canada Mortgage and Housing Corporation (CMHC)—provided \$972 and \$95 million of public funding in BC, Ontario and Alberta from 2009–2012. **In terms of efficiency**, the investment was critical in addressing the lack of resources to fund capital repairs and system upgrades in the aging social housing stock. The programs were highly relevant, timely and successful in meeting their broad objectives, and account for improvements in about 20% to 50% of the social housing in BC, Ontario and Alberta. CEAP provided grant funds for a variety of mechanical, structural and building envelope retrofits affecting two thirds of the social housing in Toronto, Calgary and Edmonton. The impact, in terms of units upgraded, was particularly significant for the non-profit and cooperative housing providers, which saw on average over 60% of their portfolio affected by program measures.

Box 8.1 Greenbrook Sustainability Project, Surrey, British Columbia
Built in 1974, Greenbrook is a public housing development owned and operated by BC Housing, consisting of 127 units in 28 townhouses that are home to 380 people. The Greenbrook sustainability project combined both building envelope replacement and energy upgrades to achieve significant energy savings and physical improvements. The use of high efficiency heating and electrical systems reduced GHG emissions by 86% in 2010 compared to the baseline recorded in 2005. The project boasts the largest residential solar panel installation in Western Canada which offsets about 10% of the site-used

(continued)

Box 8.1 (continued)

electricity and a large portion of the remaining energy consumption, resulting in a housing complex that is very close to being carbon neutral.

Source: Tsenkova and Youssef (2012)

Part of the success is attributed to the efficient management of the programs by existing federal, provincial and municipal housing institutions. The institutional framework for rapid deployment of program funds (centralized in BC versus decentralized in Ontario) left the service providers sufficient autonomy to address priority needs. Large social housing providers in Vancouver, Toronto, Calgary and Edmonton, due to their institutional capacity, were able to address in a more comprehensive manner both energy efficiency and capital improvement needs in their social housing portfolio. A more robust policy framework for energy efficiency retrofits in BC and Ontario—incorporating a range of regulatory, fiscal and institutional policy instruments—positively influenced portfolio investment strategies. In Alberta, less emphasis was placed on energy efficiency retrofits for the benefit of general renovations of the social housing stock, safety improvements and enhanced accessibility for persons with disabilities. By contrast, BC Housing developed a business model where energy efficiency was systematically pursued through partnering of CEAP capital projects with provincial sustainability initiatives (e.g. *Public Sector Energy Conservation Agreement and BC LiveSmart),* while in Ontario housing providers leveraged funding from the *Renewable Energy Initiative* and other utility managed programs to maximize the reduction in energy use and GHG emissions in the social housing sector (Box 8.1).

The effectiveness of CEAP programs was difficult to evaluate in the absence of a systematic monitoring and post-retrofit evaluation system. Nevertheless, evidence from twelve case study projects in the four cities under review demonstrates substantial improvements in the quality of social housing, targeted approaches to retrofits, integrating both mechanical and building envelope measures, and high potential for energy savings (20% to 45%). Notwithstanding the emphasis on 'best practices' in the analysis, it is evident that the programs prompted a more strategic approach to asset management and energy retrofits by major public, non-profit and

Fig. 8.1 Social Benefits by Design. *Source: Author's field visits*

cooperative housing providers. Another critical success factor was institutional innovation in BC using energy service companies (ESCOs). While the ESCO model was more expensive than the project manager/contract services model, there were value-added components including economies of scale, the 'one stop shop' approach and enhanced accountability for planning, financing and monitoring projects. The social benefits of the retrofit projects are particularly difficult to quantify, but in many cases technical measures were complemented by investment in playgrounds, community gardens and common spaces that enhance residents' quality of life and provide opportunities for community interaction. The examples below illustrate these design and community building strategies. Figure 8.1 shows a new playground built in Grant McNeil Place in Vancouver and the new tenant lounge and green rooftop garden at 42 Hubbard Street heritage building in Toronto.

The CMHC managed program targeted federal housing coops. Staff at the federal level worked hard to overcome the constraints of a decentralized model of social housing providers to ensure that program benefits were available to all. Efforts included assistance with project submissions, and monitoring of spending and site inspections to ensure consistency between planned and actual program measures. Some of the most popular retrofits, in addition to lighting—'the low hanging fruit'—were roofing, window replacement, cladding/insulation and mechanical system upgrades (boilers). Energy efficiency retrofits were supported, but this was not necessarily a priority. The cooperatives were able to address the tension between short-term affordability goals and the long-term viability of their housing stock using program funds, thus developing much-needed experience with strategic planning.

Figure 8.2 profiles the allocation of funds from the CMHC administered program to federal housing cooperatives in the four cities under review. The data illustrates the investment priorities and choices made by a variety of housing organisations measured by the cost of major retrofits. Window and door replacement consumed a considerable portion of the budget in the four cities ($11 million). In Edmonton this accounted for 43% of the total spending and for 29% of the total spending in Calgary. Roof replacement was the second most important type of retrofit ($9 million), and was particularly significant in Vancouver and Toronto. Other major

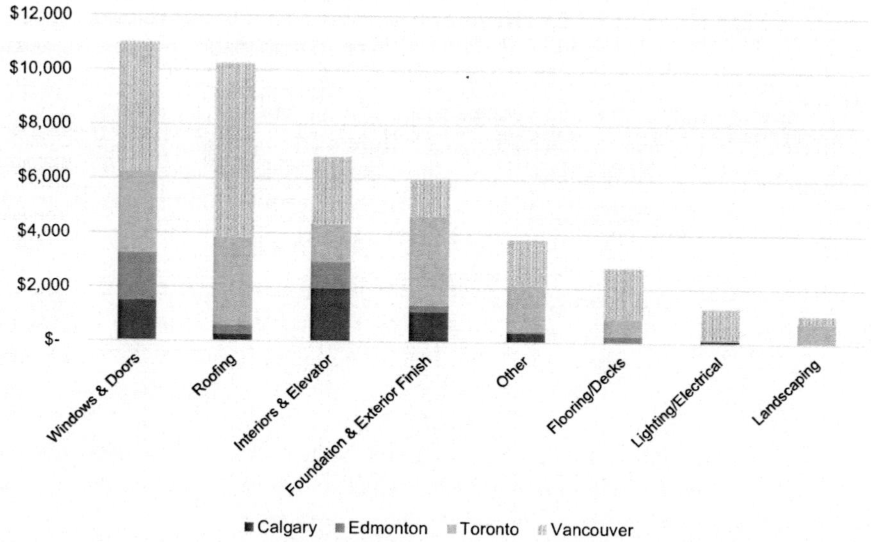

Fig. 8.2 Comparison of Retrofit and Investment Priorities—CMHC funding. Source: Interview data, CMHC Program Director, August 2012

categories of retrofits—interior upgrades and foundation work/exterior cladding/insulation—accounted for $7 million and $6 million. The first was important for cooperatives and non-profits in Calgary and Vancouver, while the second was critical for social providers in Toronto.

Regardless of the overall success of the programs, the funding only temporarily addressed the lack of resources available to maintain the social housing stock. A longer term and consistent funding model needs to be developed to ensure the sustainability of results achieved. Rent reforms and other approaches to secure long-term funding and more effective asset management practices are needed, in addition to strong political motivation to improve the quality and the energy efficiency of the sector.

8.3 Challenges of Energy Efficiency Retrofit Programs (2009–2013)

Program challenges were associated with tight timelines and difficulties in coordinating and planning strategic retrofits. Although the projects supported through CEAP were deemed 'shovel ready', housing providers and building managers had to operate within a two-year timeframe. Unexpected building envelope problems were frequently reported, resulting in cost overruns, project delays and potential loss of funding if projects were not implemented on time.

The tight deadlines for program management and administration, which given the sometimes unpredictable nature of construction work, led to program extensions and reallocation of funds for other types of measures. The reason behind the unofficial prolongation of the two-year period of the program was mainly due to the time needed for tendering and contracting retrofit work, as the delays resulted from permit applications and building inspection processes. Some of the smaller social housing organisations reportedly faced capacity constraints and difficulties in the management of construction work, contracts, and even qualifying for program funds due to complex guidelines and procedures.

One of the greatest challenges was the high cost of the program and the lack of sustainability in funding. In more comprehensive improvement and energy efficiency projects, such as those in the case studies, simple payback periods are anywhere between 39 and 67 years. Even though the financial viability and cost-benefit of these programs were not the main objectives, they highlight future economic challenges if programs need to be operated on a cost recovery principle. *Limited market penetration of energy efficiency in social housing is constrained by lack of access to capital, high risk and split incentives* (Haney et al. 2010; Jollands et al. 2010). Social housing providers face significant challenges accessing standard loans and mortgages based on cash flow and general rent revenue, making investments in energy efficient components much more challenging, given their high upfront costs, lengthy payback period and uncertainty in energy pricing. Rents in the social housing sector are often set as a percentage of household income, inclusive of utilities, so tenants do not have a direct incentive to reduce their energy consumption. While social housing providers are interested in investing in energy efficient mechanical systems, tenants often object to such measures as they create temporary inconvenience during the implementation period. Such split incentives, in addition to general behavioural failures and reluctance on behalf of consumers to adopt an energy responsible behaviour, hinder the adoption of energy efficiency measures (Moezzi 2009).

Furthermore, for a number of social housing providers, particularly in Alberta, energy efficiency was a low priority relative to other portfolio considerations. This is also true for a number of small community-based social housing organisations (non-profits and cooperatives) in BC and Ontario, which lack the institutional capacity to comprehensively plan for energy efficient retrofits due to limited, asymmetric information and other structural barriers. The physical condition of the social housing portfolio and the lack of adequate reserves to address capital needs significantly affected the implementation of the programs. *The tradeoff between energy efficient retrofits and the replacement of deteriorated mechanical and building envelope components was a major challenge of the programs*, particularly the component administered by the CMHC. Sometimes there was not enough funding to do both.

The specific retrofit measures in the case studies are diverse and illustrate the significant challenges of such programs in economic terms. *If the simple payback of energy efficiency measures is used as an overall consideration for return on investment, it will be difficult to make the case for green retrofits in the social housing sector*. Feasibility studies, however, point to significant environmental benefits resulting from reduced energy and water consumption, and reduced GHG emissions. Some of these metrics of performance, as well as the social impact measured in tenant satisfaction and improved health and wellbeing, were difficult to quantify and there was a very limited attempt to introduce a system to monitor and evaluate achieved results, even on a pilot basis.

While the greening of social housing has many benefits, the installation of green technologies is a strain on capital reserves. CEAP and REI provided an important financial boost to experimentation with sustainable design and green technologies such as solar walls/roofs and green roofs, but there were significant market barriers for effective implementation.

8.4 Success of Energy Efficiency Retrofit Programs (2014–2020)

The overview of the energy efficiency retrofit programs in the social housing sector of three provinces (Ontario, British Columbia and Alberta) in the post *Canada Economic Action Plan* period (2014–2020) illustrated how different provincial priorities and housing policies affect program design and strategies for implementation. Commitments to climate change shifted priorities towards reducing GHG emission from existing buildings as an important part in achieving environmental sustainability. Policies and funding programs that aid the retrofit of the social housing stock addressed not only environmental priorities, but also social and public health concerns. Upgrading social and affordable housing for energy efficiency reduces energy costs and contributes to Canada's mission to lower our carbon footprint for a better and greener future.

The new wave of energy retrofit programs in Toronto and Vancouver, although smaller in scope, were efficient, timely and indicated a more systematic approach. Energy audits were a standard program requirement and program design incentivized providers to minimize GHG emissions. BC Housing capital program provided specific incentives for performance targets achieved, encouraging environmental sustainability. Vancouver continued its successful collaboration with utility companies to deliver energy conservation projects and to realize British Columbia's GHG reduction goals. The energy efficiency retrofitting programs leveraged the utility companies' incentives and their expertise to ensure efficient and effective implementation of retrofits. This public-private partnership supported the financial sustainability of Vancouver's small-scale retrofits that employ currently available technologies. Collectively, the energy retrofit programs in Toronto provided $247 million to various housing providers to carry out capital repairs and system upgrades in social housing. In the process, the funding improved 13% of TCHC's portfolio and 33% of the affordable housing of non-profit and co-op sectors.

The institutional frameworks of different programs contributed to program effectiveness, ensuring equitable distribution of the limited funding. In Toronto, the City allocated two thirds of its SHARP and SHIP funding to TCHC and the rest to non-profit and co-op housing providers, which corresponds to their share of social housing. In Vancouver SHRSP funding is administered by the utility companies, while Efficiency BC reimburses projects based on their actual GHG reduction. *The execution of more comprehensive retrofits ensured economies of scale* where the project design, procurement, contract management and execution is coordinated and implemented in a timely manner. TCHC and BC Housing had established relationship with contractors and sound project management systems. The energy efficiency audit requirement was beneficial in packaging types of retrofits with the highest environmental benefits—reduction in energy costs and GHG emissions. Some innovative projects supporting comprehensive retrofits to passive house standards emerged (see Box 8.2).

Box 8.2 Ken Soble Tower's Passive House Retrofit, Hamilton, Ontario

Ken Soble Tower is Canada's first Passive House residential tower retrofit. CityHousing Hamilton led the project to create 146 new affordable rental studio-and-one-bedroom apartments for seniors at below market rents (CityHousing Hamilton n.d.). The funding includes $6.3 million from the National Housing Co-Investment Fund and $3.7 million from the Affordable Housing Innovation Fund (Canada Mortgage and Housing Corporation 2019). The partnership involves CityHousing Hamilton, the federal government, the city of Hamilton and the Federation of Canadian Municipalities who provides funding via the Green Municipal Fund (O'Reilly 2019).

Ken Soble Tower is retrofitted according to EnerPHit standards. Major components involve envelope upgrade, system modernization, building exterior R38 overcladding equipped with rainscreen and rock wool insulation, Passive House-standard windows. In terms of mechanical systems, the

(continued)

Box 8.2 (continued)
building has a centralized HVAC equipped with cooling risers and air handling units with direct ducting into individual apartments for in-suite temperature control. All common areas of the building are accessible with ageing in place in mind. Residents enjoy a new solarium and green roof with view of the Hamilton Harbour. Based on the National Energy Code for Buildings, the retrofitted building will demonstrate 75% reduction in energy use and 88% reduction in GHG emissions (Canada Mortgage and Housing Corporation 2019). During peak periods, the energy required to heat or cool a unit will be equivalent to what is needed to operate three incandescent light bulbs (ERA Architects n.d.).

Source: ERA Architects (n.d.)

The review of this new wave of programs illustrated the **importance of partnerships** through public, private and non-profit collaboration as a strategy for implementation. Notwithstanding the complexities of these collaborations, they provided critical opportunities to improve the social housing sector through coordinated investment in different types of retrofits aligning them with program requirements and metrics of performance. BC Housing is collaborating with The Pembina Institute to adapt Energiespong model of a complete retrofit that promises to foster innovation, reduce construction time and deliver net-zero energy performance for existing residential buildings (Box 8.3). To date, 5,000 houses have been retrofitted to net-zero energy using this model in the Netherlands and another 14,400 planned for retrofit (Energiesprong n.d.-a, -b).

Box 8.3 Adapting the Energiesprong Model in British Columbia
Energiespong is a Dutch award-winning model of a complete retrofit and funding approach that promises to foster innovation, reduce construction time and deliver net-zero energy performance for existing buildings. The Pembina Institute, supported through CMHC Innovation Lab Grant, is the leading organization bringing this model to BC (Energiesprong n.d.-c). The Affordable Housing Renewal pilot aggregates the demand for energy retrofit and amalgamates contracts for a common archetype of building. Through competitive procurement processes, aggregation is expected to deliver more innovative solutions that require less construction time and produce more energy and cost savings. With large contracts, economies of scale promise efficiency and cost reduction. One innovation is prefabrication that can significantly cut down installation time and effort when done for a sizeable number of buildings (Heerema 2017). Fabricated components such as structural insulated panels make this solution for aggregation of energy retrofitting in BC viable. Computer models for individual buildings could be made with

(continued)

Box 8.3 (continued)
3D laser scanning technique to enable precise fabrication of insulated panels for better air tightness and moisture resistance.

The Pembina Institute estimates that 2500 housing units could be included in the first pilot (Frappé-Sénéclauze et al. 2017). The retrofit into net-zero energy and zero-carbon developments, could lead to energy reduction of 250,000 GJ and 7000 to 10,000 tonnes of CO_2 equivalent per year. For low-rise apartments built prior to 2000, the post-retrofit energy savings could be $13,300 to $29,600 over 25 years for each unit. With the aggregation method, the average retrofit cost per square metre is $1500 compared to $2500.

Source: The Pembina Institute, 2018.

Institutional partnerships capitalised on the effective role of the public sector in the mobilization of resources, the efficiencies of private agencies in the development process (design, build) and the hybridity of the non-profit institutions (management, service delivery). In both cities the institutional structure for program administration capitalised on institutional arrangements set up for the retrofit programs under the previous *Canada Economic Action Plan.* Such continuity makes the follow up smaller programs more efficient. An overall attempt to ensure fairness and consistency in program funding allocation was evident with a specific emphasis on the involvement of smaller non-profit and cooperative housing providers. While market penetration of retrofit technologies is still small, the institutional frameworks benefit from partnerships with a strong public sector lead. Both approaches produced successes as Toronto's decentralized method consolidated many critical functions in a key organization for higher efficiency, consistency and more support dedicated to smaller housing providers. Vancouver's strategy utilized the competitive advantages of a centralised administration by BC Housing working in partnership with other sectors to deliver accessible retrofit options.

8.5 Challenges of Energy Efficiency Retrofit Programs (2014–2020)

The research in Toronto and Vancouver indicated that with multiple funding opportunities for energy retrofits, each with its own set of criteria and administrative processes to follow, small and less experienced housing providers may have had a hard time accessing these funds. Large providers such as TCHC and BC Housing are often more well-versed with the nuances of different programs as well as their criteria and are able to combine various sources of funding to finance more extensive retrofits. *Non-profit housing providers are likely to prioritize energy conservation measures that have shorter payback periods* such as lighting over large-ticket items such as cladding or window replacement, as illustrated in the City Park Coop case studies. Despite the differences in the way these energy retrofit initiatives were set up, the funding sources were not necessarily reliable. Many of the programs discussed were one-off with no commitment for renewal. The *Renewable Investment Initiative* in Ontario was cancelled, so the opportunity to scale up innovative projects, such as Solar Walls remains limited. This has created tremendous difficulty for funding administrators to determine criteria for distribution of limited resources. Some affordable housing projects may be in need of funding for critical structural upgrades that may not result in energy efficiency. It is also a balancing act between equity in funding allocation vs effectiveness to insure impactful retrofits.

As the featured retrofit projects suggest, many building components in affordable housing developments were costly and not necessarily viable to retrofit in terms of simple return on investment. Building envelope retrofits, despite their high contribution to reduction of energy consumption and GHG emissions, were very capital intensive with a simple pay back exceeding 100 years. ***Developing new technologies and methodologies will be essential to solve the economic challenge of retrofitting affordable housing for energy efficiency.*** For housing organisations, any cost savings as a result of energy retrofits will lessen the amount of subsidy provinces provide (Frappé-Sénéclauze et al. 2017). This adversely affects the post-retrofit cash flow for housing providers as financial savings due to capital-intensive retrofits are registered as reduction in equity rather than reduction in operating expenses, making the pay-back period for such projects even longer.

Institutional partnerships for program implementation need strong leadership, often from a city-based housing agency that has the ability to coordinate finance, manage projects in a dynamic real estate environment and deliver on time and budget. *Research findings indicated that the implementation process relied on senior government funding (federal and provincial) for capital costs, but more importantly on predictable and stable source of funding.* Changes in provincial governments in Ontario and Alberta resulted in cancellation of programs with a negative impact over the social housing sector. In Ontario, funding from the province's carbon market was a good demonstration of effective use of carbon taxes and financial innovation to support retrofits. However, it was also highly susceptible to changes in the province's political leadership. Following the change of government in 2018 and the cancellation of the cap-and-trade program, many of the programs had their funding reduced or withdrawn altogether. In Alberta programs targeting energy efficiency were discontinued due to government changes. *In summary, carbon pricing and environmental policies are effective in curbing GHG emissions, but they do not provide a stable source of funding for energy retrofits in the social housing sector.* Ontario's cancellation of their cap-and-trade program illustrates this point. The sector needs a sustainable public sector commitment that recognises the synergy of environmental, economic and social benefits.

8.6 Key Recommendations

An important finding from this first assessment of decade-long energy efficiency retrofit programs in the Canadian social housing sector is that the implementation is a long-term process that will take decades to address the existing gap. The challenges are particularly significant in large Canadian cities. *Effective and efficient implementation needs to builds on effective partnerships of different levels of government, robust and sustained financial support, alignment of policies and institutional commitment to increase its outreach and deliver results.* Such complexity by design makes statements on 'what works' and 'what does not' challenging (Tsenkova 2018).

There is substantial literature identifying barriers to energy efficiency retrofits and the appropriate policy responses to overcoming these barriers (Haney et al. 2010; Moezzi 2009). A major distinction is made between regulatory, fiscal and financial policy instruments to address market barriers and market failures, both of which contribute to explaining the energy efficiency gap (International Energy Agency 2007). Energy efficiency investments are often irreversible with a fair amount of uncertainty about both the benefits and energy savings of new technology. Accordingly, customers and investors show a high degree of risk aversion in their decision-making resulting in maintaining the status quo and resistance to change (Farsi 2010). Added to the irreversibility and uncertainty in investment returns is the preference to select measures that offer a short payback over other strategic options that may have better advantages over the long-term (Jackson 2010). A successful strategy that promotes energy efficiency retrofits is one that combines "sticks" (regulations) with "carrots" (incentives) and "tambourines" (awareness raising campaigns) (Kaufman and Palmer 2011; Tsenkova 2003).

Financial incentives fall into two broad categories: investment subsidies and soft loans. Such subsidies aim at reducing the investment cost of retrofits and shorten payback time, thus allowing social housing providers to overcome one of the main market barriers/failures to energy efficiency investment: access to capital. The most common measure to overcome this barrier is through soft loans, or by third-party financing via ESCOs energy service companies that are reimbursed by energy savings made, or special purpose funds, revolving funds, credit lines and loan guarantees (Sarkar and Singh 2010).

Fiscal incentives include measures to reduce the annual income tax paid by providers who invest in energy efficiency renovations, such as accelerated depreciation, tax credits and tax deductions, tax reduction when purchasing energy efficient equipment or when investing to improve energy efficiency in buildings (e.g. GST exemption). Such incentives are considered less costly for public budget. Preference for economic instruments (subsidies and taxes) over command-and-control instruments (e.g. performance standards) has been made in the literature with respect to innovation in energy efficiency and contribution to environmental policy goals (Noailly and Batrakova 2010). Complementary to the above policy instruments is the *category of information, capacity-building programs and educational measures*.

Information programs typically provide information about potential energy savings or examples of energy savings in order to increase awareness and motivation for energy efficiency investments (Kikuchi et al. 2009). Capacity-building programs usually take the form of training programs and 'energy retrofits' counselling.

This first systematic evaluation of energy efficiency retrofits in the social housing sector of Canadian cities indicates that federal and provincial governments have adopted an incremental model of policy design and implementation. *It proceeds through 'trial and error', often with complex and decentralised relationships at different levels of policy-making and implementation. The outcomes in the social housing system do not imply fundamentally new approaches, but a response to problems of lower quality, deferred maintenance and high energy intensity.* While this represents 'sensible politics' resulting in strategic change in the sector during the CEAP policy cycle, the 'trial and error' policy design that defines the new wave of programs and investment is constrained by political shifts and lack of stability in funding. As such, it becomes less effective and can be defined as 'muddling through', where positive outcomes can be reversed over time due to lack of continuity and institutional commitment (Tsenkova 2009). The result in the social housing system in Alberta is an illustration of this reversal back to the 'status quo'.

It is beyond the scope of this research to formulate comprehensive recommendations to enhance the potential of energy efficiency retrofits in social housing. **However, future programs need to incorporate the following key directions for transformative change**:

1. The federal and provincial governments need to secure funding for the continuation of retrofit programs with well-defined program targets that link general quality improvements in the social housing sector to energy efficiency retrofits. It is important to continue to address the funding gap in the sector, as well as to provide a more structured policy framework for energy efficiency in order to avoid the negative effect of 'start-and-stop' programs. The program needs to provide a long-term sustainable source of funding with clear quantitative targets for energy efficiency improvement and metrics of performance.
2. Provincial governments, in partnership with financial institutions, need to identify a suite of economic incentives such as soft loans, low cost secondary mortgages, credit lines and loan guarantees to allow leveraging of additional funds for renewal and energy efficiency retrofits by social housing providers. These will be different across provinces depending on provincial priorities, acceptance by the housing finance market and the diverse institutional landscape of social housing providers across Canada. The issues are particularly critical for small social housing providers in the non-profit and cooperative sector that do not have the capacity to raise funds for critical upgrades, nor the institutional expertise to deal with complex retrofit programming and budgeting operations.
3. Provincial governments, in partnership with the largest social housing providers, need to provide systematic training and capacity building to improve the governance and decision-making around capital planning projects. The large investment opportunity in the last three years increased accountability and fostered new

practices in the housing sector (e.g. ESCOs) as well as documented the value added approach of strategic packaging of retrofit measures. Managing large capital projects raised the credibility of the sector and its capacity to deliver successful retrofit programs. Small non-profit and cooperative housing providers would benefit from the accumulated experience in managing and executing retrofit programs in the future.

4. Federal and provincial governments, in partnership with the largest social housing providers, need to disseminate evidence from ex-post evaluation of select best practices to overcome capacity and information constraints in the sector. They should develop effective training programs for tenants based on social marketing that has the potential of triggering energy responsive behaviour, reducing consumption by 20% and addressing split incentives. It is important to move beyond the present delivery mechanisms in the form of 'one-way' assistance to a model that includes tenants and low-income households as local program agents.
5. Federal and provincial government agencies need to commit to monitoring and evaluating energy retrofit programs. Comprehensive reports and studies are needed to evaluate the success and failures of the programs as well as the outputs, results achieved and actions implemented. These are non-existent and there is even less information on the impacts in terms of post-retrofit costs and energy savings. This may be explained by evaluation difficulties specific to 'low income' programs such as obstacles for data collection, lack of official data, and specific program targets and monitoring requirements. Such post-retrofit evaluations of the recent experience in the social housing sector would be useful as a guide in promoting successful and reliable retrofit strategies for the rest of the residential sector.
6. Establishing an institutional framework at the municipal level building on partnerships for efficient and effective program administration is highly recommended. Such key organization can provide one-stop services relating to the specific energy retrofit packages, procurement, contract administration and execution that allows smaller non-profit providers to capitalise on opportunities. Institutional support for complete retrofits and a funding approach that fosters innovation, reduces construction time and promotes net-zero energy performance for existing housing could make a difference. Aggregation of contracts for a common archetype of building (apartments & townhomes) promises economies of scale, efficiency and cost reduction.

This research of social housing energy efficient retrofit programs in Canadian cities illustrates the environmental, economic and social benefits of comprehensive retrofits (see Tsenkova 2018). It also illustrates the challenges affecting this process. *In the context of post-pandemic economic recovery, there is an excellent opportunity to invest in a greener and more inclusive future.* In the affordable housing sector this is an opportunity for policy makers and industry players to reorganize their institutional relationship to improve workflow that will ensure the efficiency and effectiveness of energy retrofit projects (Tsenkova 2019).

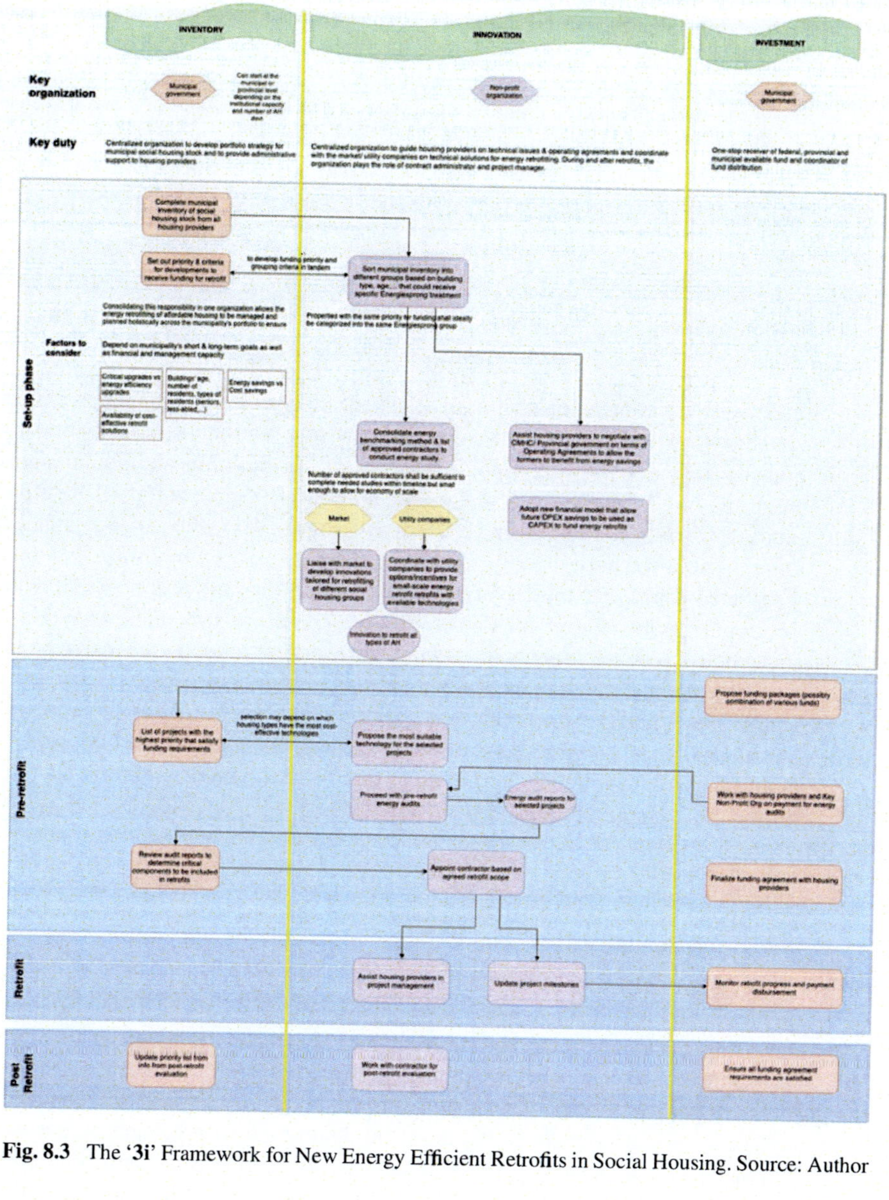

Fig. 8.3 The '**3i**' Framework for New Energy Efficient Retrofits in Social Housing. Source: Author

The '3i' framework mapped out in Fig. 8.3 proposes a program structure, which can do just that (see Tran and Tsenkova 2019). The main challenges are grouped in three domains—lack of institutional capacity of housing providers to navigate the administrative processes, lack of economically viable energy retrofitting technologies and lack of funding. The new **3i'** institutional framework is anchored by three main work streams—inventory, innovation and investment. Each of these work streams has a key organization that provides one-stop services centralizing functions to allow more effective management of processes driven by a more holistic and comprehensive vision for sustainable delivery. Streamlining energy retrofit projects into three main processes enables more players to be involved and the development of partnerships for implementation. This approach is a combination of Toronto's effective centralization practice and Vancouver's successful partnership in managing and delivering energy retrofit projects.

8.6.1 *Inventory*

The inventory stream deals with all administrative processes, starting with a consolidated complete inventory of all social housing within a municipality from all housing providers with complete information on building and tenant parameters and providing administrative supports to all housing organizations' efforts to obtain funding for retrofit. This can be used to design a portfolio strategy that sets out criteria and ultimately priority for funding. It can assure that limited resources are distributed fairly and effectively among housing projects and no eligible housing developments are left out due to their housing providers' lack of capacity. Pooling all social housing developments in a municipality allows for comprehensive planning of resources and the economies of scale encourage more participation from the private sector. Municipalities can determine the criteria in accordance with short and long-term goals for affordable housing and building energy efficiency as well as their financial and management capacity to ensure flexibility in determining the priority of projects to receive funding for energy retrofit.

8.6.2 *Innovation*

A non-profit organization can manage the innovation stream. It can be responsible for technical issues including coordination of contractors for energy audit reports, consolidation of energy saving upgrades offered by utility companies and work with industry partners to develop tailor made and economically sustainable retrofit solutions for various housing types. As such, the non-profit organization needs to have strong technical capacity and the necessary skills to engage with both public and private sectors effectively. The key organization for this stream is a blend of the BC Non-profit Housing Association and the Pembina Institute working to bring the Dutch Energiesprong to British Columbia's social housing sector. To address the low economic viability of some retrofits, the Energiesprong methodology is integrated into this stream based on coordination with industry to develop innovative solutions for a sizeable number of affordable housing projects.

8.6.3 Investment

The perpetual lack of funding for affordable housing retrofit is addressed in the investment stream. The experience of the City of Toronto and TCHC with programs and project implementation suggests that municipal governments can become the one-stop receiver of all funding sources. Their knowledge of the social housing conditions as custodians of the 'inventory' stream combined with thorough knowledge of program requirements can ensure equitable and targeted allocation of funding. This reverses the current approach where housing providers must navigate requirements from multiple funding initiatives and apply for each of them individually. The complexity of administrative processes is a deterrent for more comprehensive retrofits. To improve the financial viability of energy retrofits, housing providers need to have predictable financial framework allowing benefits from energy savings to be reinvested in the portfolio. Capital expenditures (capex) are reserved for upgrades critical to the integrity and longevity of buildings. Typically, such capital expenditure in energy retrofits produce savings in maintenance and utility costs that are part of buildings' operating expenditures (opex), but they have long payback period.

References

Brophy, H., Jamasb, H., Platchkov, L., & Pollitt, M. (2010). Demand-side Management Strategies and the Residential Sector: Lessons from International Experience. In *EPRG Working Paper 1034; Cambridge Working Paper in Economics 1060*: Electricity Policy Research Group. Cambridge: University of Cambridge.

Canada Mortgage & Housing Corporation. (2019, May 21). *First Ever Passive House High-Rise Retrofit in Canada Will Create More Affordable Housing for Seniors in Hamilton*. Retrieved from Canada Mortgage & Housing Company. https://www.cmhc-schl.gc.ca/en/media-newsroom/news-releases/2019/first-ever-passive-house-high-rise-retrofit-canada-create-more-affordable-housing-senior-hamilton

CityHousing Hamilton. (n.d.). *500 MacNab*. Retrieved from CityHousing Hamilton. http://www.cityhousinghamilton.com/page1.aspx?page=MacNabPropDev&tab=6&menu=672

Energiesprong. (n.d.-a). *About Energiesprong*. Retrieved from Energiesprong: https://energiesprong.org/about/

Energiesprong. (n.d.-b). *Energiesprong*. Retrieved June 30, 2019, from Energiesprong: https://energiesprong.org/

Energiesprong. (n.d.-c). *British Columbia*. Retrieved June 30, 2019, from Energiesprong: https://energiesprong.org/country/british-columbia/

ERA Architects. (n.d.). *Ken Soble Tower*. Retrieved from ERA Architects: http://www.eraarch.ca/project/ken-soble-tower-transformation/

Farsi, M. (2010). Risk aversion and willingness to pay for energy efficient systems in rental apartments. *Energy Policy, 38*(6), 3078–3088.

Frappé-Sénéclauze, T.-P., Heerema, D., & Bobyn, D. (2017). *Aggregation of energy retrofits in affordable housing: Opportunities and challenges in adapting the Energiesprong model in B.C.* Pembina Institute.

Haney, A., Jamasb, T., Platchkov, L., & Pollitt, M. (2010). Demand-side Management Strategies and the Residential Sector: Lessons from International Experience. In *EPRG Working Paper 1034; Cambridge Working Paper in Economics 1060*: Electricity Policy Research Group. Cambridge: University of Cambridge.

Heerema, D. (2017, July 19). *Better homes, lower costs, less pollution: The Energiesprong model and B.C.*

International Energy Agency. (2007). *Mind the Gap: Quantifying Principal-Agent Problems in Energy Efficiency*. Paris: OECD Publishing.

Jackson, J. (2010). Promoting energy efficiency investments with risk management decision tools. *Energy Policy, 38*(8), 3865–3873.

Jollands, N., Waide, P., Ellis, M., Onoda, T., Laustsen, J., Tanaka, K., et al. (2010). The 25 IEA energy efficiency policy recommendations to the G8 gleneagles plan of action. *Energy Policy, 38*(11), 6409–6418.

Kaufman, N., & Palmer, K. (2011). Energy efficiency program evaluations: opportunities for learning and inputs to incentive mechanisms. *Energy Efficiency*, 1–26.

Kikuchi, E., Bristow, D., & Kennedy, C. (2009). Evaluation of region-specific residential energy systems for GHG reductions: Case studies in Canadian cities. *Energy Policy, 37*(4), 1257–1266.

Moezzi, M. (2009). *Behavioral assumptions in energy efficiency potential studies*. California: California Institute for Energy and Environment CIEE.

Noailly, J., & Batrakova, S. (2010). Stimulating energy-efficient innovations in the Dutch building sector: Empirical evidence from patent counts and policy lessons. *Energy Policy, 38*(12), 7803–7817.

O'Reilly, D. (2019, March 29). *Hamilton's Ken Soble Tower rebirth a Passive House first*. Retrieved from Daily Commericial News by ConstructConnect: https://canada.constructconnect.com/dcn/news/projects/2019/03/hamiltons-ken-soble-tower-rebirth-passive-house-first

Pembina Institute. (2018). *Affordable housing renewal: Retrofits at scale - workshop summary*. Pembina Institute.

Sarkar, A., & Singh, J. (2010). Financing energy efficiency in developing countries--lessons learned and remaining challenges. *Energy Policy, 38*(10), 5560–5571.

Stephenson, J., Barton, B., Carrington, G., Gnoth, D., Lawson, R., & Thorsnes, P. (2010). Energy cultures: A framework for understanding energy behaviours. *Energy Policy, 38*(10), 6120–6129.

Tran, J., & Tsenkova, S. (2019). Policy design of energy efficiency retrofitting programs in Vancouver and Toronto: What next? Paper presented at the ENHR Conference "Housing for the Next European Social Model", August 27-30, 2019; Athens: Greece.

Tsenkova, S. (2003). Housing policy matters: The reform path in Central and Eastern Europe: Policy convergence? In S. Tsenkova & S. Lowe (Eds.), *Housing change in Central and Eastern Europe* (pp. 193–205). Aldershot: Ashgate Publishing Limited.

Tsenkova, S. (2009). *Housing reforms in post-socialist Europe. Lost In transition*. Heidelberg: Springer.

Tsenkova, S. (2013). *Retrofits for the future: Affordable housing and energy efficiency programs in Canada*. Calgary: University of Calgary. Retrieved February 10, 2019, from https://ucalgary.ca/cities/files/cities/EnergyRetrofitsTsenkova2013.pdf

Tsenkova, S. (2018). Transformative change: Energy-efficiency and social housing retrofits in Canadian cities. *Urban Research and Practice, 11*(3), 263–274.

Tsenkova, S. (2019). Social housing on trial: Institutions + policy design. *Urban Research and Practice, 12*(1), 1–6.

Tsenkova, S., & Youssef, K. (2012). Canada: Energy efficiency retrofits – policy solutions for sustainable social housing. In N. Nieber, S. Tsenkova, V. Gruis, & A. van Hal (Eds.), *Energy efficiency in housing management* (pp. 209–231). London: Routledge.

Annex

Profiles of Social Housing Retroft Projects in Toronto and Vancouver

A.1 Glamorgan Avenue Project, Toronto

Table A.1 Project profile

Grant	SHAIP
Development name	Kennedy Glamorgan
Address	6 Glamorgan Ave
Housing provider	Toronto community housing corporation
Year of construction[a]	1971
Building type[b]	High-rise apartment building
Wheelchair accessibility[b]	No
No. of Storeys[b]	12
No. of Units[b]	184
Total funding	$8,032,855
Program	SHAIP

(continued)

S. Tsenkova, *Energy Efficient Affordable Housing*,
https://doi.org/10.1007/978-3-030-69563-7

Table A.1 (continued)

Grant	SHAIP
Funding per unit	$43,656.82
Rent structure[c]	182 RGI units

[a]PMC Engineering Solutions (2018), p. 8
[b]Toronto Community Housing Corporation (2009a)
[c]PMC Engineering Solutions (2018), p. 12

Table A.2 Types of energy retrofits: cost, incentives from utility companies and funding received

Type of Retrofit	Retrofit cost ($)	Incentives[a] ($)	Other Funding Sources ($)	SHAIP Funding[b]	% Funding
Mechanical					
Heating and domestic hot water system upgrade	720,000[c]	8243	–	711,757	8.9%
Heating terminal unit upgrade	672,259[c]	1717	–	670,542	8.3%
Makeup air unit upgrade	600,000[c]	1199	–	598,801	7.5%
Building automation system upgrade	75,000[d]	343	–	74,657	0.9%
Non-mechanical					
Over cladding	2,206,750[d]	–	–	2,206,750	27.5%
Window retrofit	1,438,500[d]	–	–	1,438,500	17.9%
Lighting retrofit	184,000[d]	12,216	–	171,784	2.1%
Others					
Other costs	2,517,246		357,182	2,160,064[e]	26.9%
Total	8,413,755[d]	23,718	357,182[d]	8,032,855[b]	

[a]PMC Engineering Solutions (2018), p. 12
[b]Figures are calculated based on assumption that the retrofit costs that are not covered by the incentives from utility companies are funded by the city under SHAIP
[c]City of Toronton, 2018
[d]Figure is calculated as the remainder of total retrofit cost after deducting SHAIP funding and utility incentives
[e]Figure is calculated as the remainder of total SHAIP funding after deducting funding on energy conservation measures

Table A.3 Energy consumption before and after energy retrofit works and projected savings per annum

	Pre-retrofit (2016–2018)[a]	Post-retrofit[b]	Projected Savings
Electricity			
Usage (kWh)	1,472,433	1,283,299	189,134[c]
Cost of use ($)	202,038	176,562	25,475.82[d]
CO_2 emission (tonnes)	118	103	15[e]
Gas			
Usage (m^3.)	367,185	96,185	271,000[c]
Cost of use ($)	107,249	29,546	77,703.18[e]
CO_2 emission (tonnes)	693	179	514[e]

(continued)

Table A.3 (continued)

	Pre-retrofit (2016–2018)[a]	Post-retrofit[b]	Projected Savings
Total cost of use ($)	309,286	206,107	103,179[c]
Total CO_2 emission	811	282	529[c]

[a]PMC Engineering Solutions (2018), pp. 23–24
[b]Figures are calculated based on pre-retrofit and savings data.
[c]City of Toronton, 2018
[d]Figures are calculated based on energy unit rates (PMC Engineering Solutions (2018), p. 23)
[e]Figure does not include other costs in addition to the energy conservation measures retrofit costs

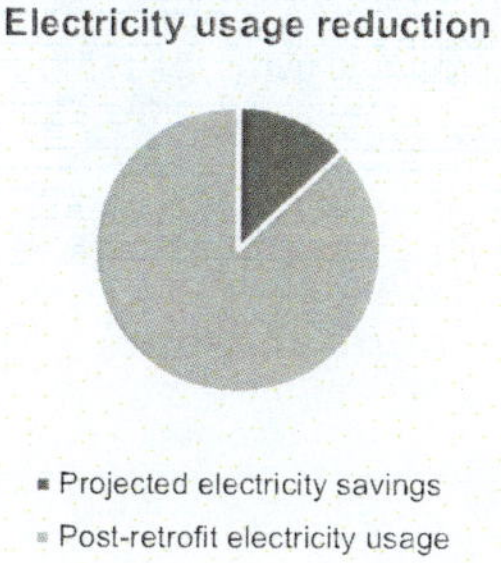

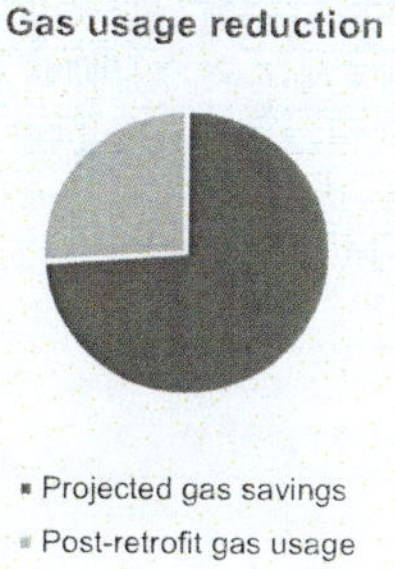

Table A.4 Projected cost and energy savings and anticipated payback per retrofit type

Type of retrofit	Projected annual savings[a] Projected gas savings (m^3)	Projected electricity savings (kWh)	GHG savings (tonnes)	Cost savings ($)	Retrofit cost ($)	Anticipated simple payback[b] (years)
Mechanical						
Heating and domestic hot water system upgrade	75,475	6949	143.1	22,999	720,000[a]	31.3
Heating terminal unit upgrade	15,724	1448	29.8	4791	672,259[a]	140.3
Makeup air unit upgrade	9981	2011	21.2	3910	600,000[c]	153.5
Building automation system upgrade	3145	290	8.7	1657	75,000[c]	45.3
Non-mechanical						
Over cladding	109,838	10,112	208.2	33,470	2,206,750[c]	65.9
Window retrofit	56,837	5233	107.7	17,319	1,438,500[c]	83.1
Lighting retrofit	–	163,091	10.4	19,033	184,000[c]	9.7
Total	271,000	189,134	529.1	103,179	5,896,509[d]	

[a]City of Toronton, 2018
[b]Figures are calculated by dividing the Retrofit Cost by the Annual Cost Savings
[c]Figure is calculated as the remainder of total retrofit cost after deducting SHAIP funding and utility incentives
[d]Figure does not include other costs in addition to the energy conservation measures retrofit costs

A.2 Falstaff Avenue Project, Toronto

Table A.5 Project profile

Grant	SHAIP
Development name	Jane Falstaff
Address	40 Falstaff avenue
Housing provider	Toronto community housing corporation
Year of construction[a]	1970
Building type[b]	High-rise apartment building
Wheelchair accessibility[c]	Yes
No. of Storeys[b]	19
No. of Units[d]	224
Total funding[d]	$12,464,821
Program	SHAIP
Funding per unit	$55,646.52
Rent structure[d]	224 RGI units

[a]PMC Engineering Services (2018), p. 8
[b]Figures are calculated based on assumption that the retrofit costs that are not covered by the incentives from utility companies are funded by the city under SHAIP
[c]Toronto Community Housing Corporation (2009b)
[d]Figures are calculated based on assumption that the retrofit costs that are not covered by the incentives from utility companies are funded by the city under SHAIP

Table A.6 Types of energy retrofits: costs, eligible incentives from utility companies and funding received

	Retrofit cost ($)	Incentives[a] ($)	Other funding sources ($)	SHAIP funding[b] ($)	% SHAIP funding
Mechanical					
Heating and DHW system upgrade	600,000[c]	13,580	–	586,420	4.7%

(continued)

Table A.6 (continued)

	Retrofit cost ($)	Incentives[a] ($)	Other funding sources ($)	SHAIP funding[b] ($)	% SHAIP funding
Heating terminal unit upgrade	703,176[d]	2829	–	700,347	5.6%
Makeup air unit upgrade	300,000[c]	1290	–	298,710	2.4%
Building automation system upgrade	75,000[c]	566	–	74,434	0.6%
Non-mechanical					
Over cladding	3,600,750[c]	–	–	3,600,750	28.9%
Window retrofit	2,545,000[c]	–	–	2,545,000	20.4%
Lighting retrofit	224,000[c]	566	–	223,434	1.8%
Other					
Other costs	5,162,245	–	726,519	4,435,726[e]	35.6%
Total	13,210,171[c]	18,831	726,519[d]	12,464,821[f]	

[a]PMC Engineering Services (2018), p. 12
[b]Figures are calculated based on assumption that the retrofit costs that are not covered by the incentives from utility companies are funded by the city under SHAIP
[c]Figure is calculated as the remainder of total retrofit cost after deducting SHAIP funding and utility incentives
[d]Figure is calculated as the remainder of total retrofit cost after deducting SHAIP funding and utility incentives
[e]Figure is calculated as the remainder of total SHAIP funding after deducting funding on energy conservation measures
[f]Figures are calculated based on assumption that the retrofit costs that are not covered by the incentives from utility companies are funded by the city under SHAIP

Table A.7 Energy consumption before and after energy retrofit works and projected savings per annum

	Pre-retrofit (2016–2018)[a]	Post-retrofit[b]	Projected savings
Electricity			
Usage (kWh)	1,701,020	1,478,876	222,144[c]
Cost of use ($)	247,858	215,489	32,369[b,d]
CO2 emission (tonnes)	136	118	18[e]
Gas			
Usage (cu.m.)	521,417	130,379	391,038[c]
Cost of use ($)	170,843	42,719	128,125[e]
CO_2 emission (tonnes)	984	246	738[e]
Total cost of use ($)	418,701	258,207	160,494[c]
Total CO_2 emission	1121	365	756[c]

[a]PMC Engineering Services (2018), pp. 23–24
[b]Figures are calculated based on pre-retrofit and savings data
[c]Figure is calculated as the remainder of total retrofit cost after deducting SHAIP funding and utility incentives
[d]Figures are calculated based on energy unit rates (PMC Engineering Solutions (2018), p. 23)
[e]Internat Energy Solutions (2016a), p. 4

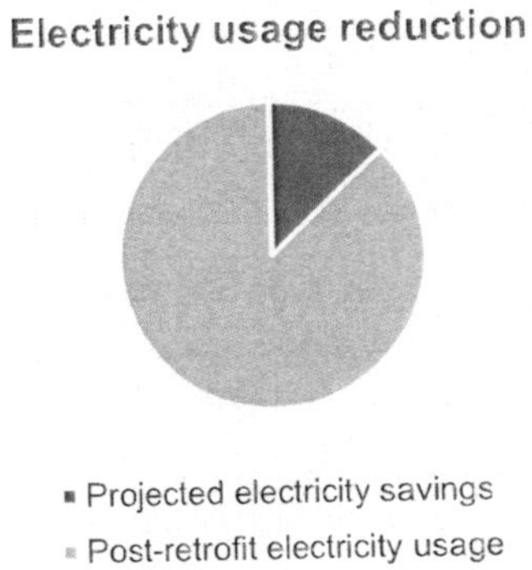

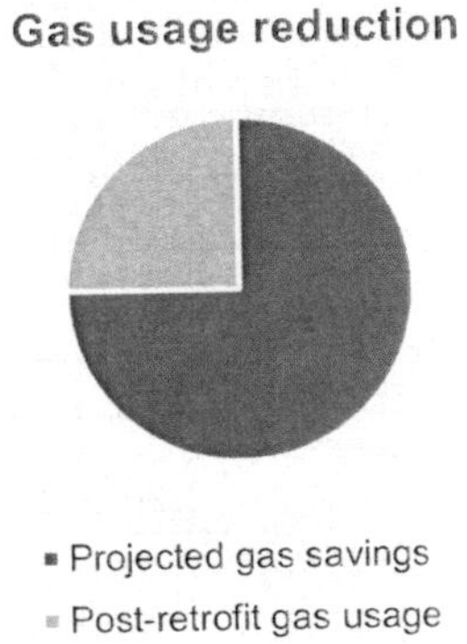

Table A.8 Projected cost and energy savings and anticipated payback per retrofit type

Type of retrofit	Projected annual Savings[a]				Retrofit cost ($)	Anticipated simple payback[b] (years)
	Projected gas savings (m^3)	Projected electricity savings (kWh)	GHG savings (tonnes)	Cost savings ($)		
Mechanical						
Heating and domestic hot water system upgrade	109,845	25,961	210	39,774	600,000[c]	17.2
Heating terminal unit upgrade	22,884	5409	44	8286	703,176[a]	84.9
Makeup air unit upgrade	11,157	1743	21	3910	300,000[c]	169.4
Building automation system upgrade	4577	1082	9	1657	75,000[c]	7.2
Non-mechanical						
Over cladding	131,622	31,108	251	47,659	3,600,750[c]	30.4
Window retrofit	110,953	26,223	212	40,175	2,545,000[c]	55.0
Lighting retrofit	–	130,618	10	19,033	224,000[c]	4.6
Total	391,038	222,144	756	160,494	8,047,926[d]	

[a]Figure is calculated as the remainder of total retrofit cost after deducting SHAIP funding and utility incentives
[b]Figures are calculated by dividing the Retrofit Cost by the Annual Cost Savings
[c]Figure is calculated as the remainder of total retrofit cost after deducting SHAIP funding and utility incentives
[d]Figure does not include other costs in addition to the energy conservation measures retrofit costs

A.3 City Park Co-operative, Toronto

Table A.9 Project profile

Grant	SHARP
Development name	City Park co-operative
Address	484 church street
Housing provider	City Park
Year of construction[a]	1954
Building type[b]	High rise apartment building
Bedrooms[b]	Studio, 1–2 bedrooms
Storeys[b]	14
No. of Units[c]	256
Total funding[c]	$1,380,917
Program	SHARP
Funding per unit	
Rent structure[c]	Some RGI units[d]

[a]Internat Energy Solutions (2016a), p. 4
[b]Renewable Energy Measure REM.2 in Energy Audit Report
[c]Figures are calculated based on assumption that the retrofit costs that are not covered by the incentives from utility companies are funded by the city under SHAIP
[d]484 Church Street is one of the three buildings within the City Park Cooperative complex with 395 RGI units

Table A.10 Energy retrofits: costs, eligible incentives from utility companies funding received

Type of retrofit	Retrofit cost ($)[a]	Incentives ($)[b]	SHARP funding[c] ($)	% funding
Renewable energy				
Solar wall[d]	53,697	–	53,697	3.9%
Mechanical				
Heating and domestic hot water system upgrade[e]	713,432	24,584	688,848	49.9%
Building automation system upgrade[b]	65,000	–	65,000	4.6%
Non-mechanical				

(continued)

Table A.10 (continued)

Type of retrofit	Retrofit cost ($)[a]	Incentives ($)[b]	SHARP funding[c] ($)	% funding
Lighting retrofit[f]	27,858	11,035	16,823	1.2%
Others			–	
Other costs	556,549	–	556,549[g]	39.3%
Total	1,416,536	35,619	1,380,917	

[a]Internat Energy Solutions (2016a), pp. 6–8
[b]Building Renewal Measure BRM.6 in Energy Audit Report
[c]Figures are calculated based on assumption that the retrofit costs that are not covered by the incentives from utility companies are funded by the city under SHARP
[d]Renewable Energy Measure REM.2 in Energy Audit Report
[e]Energy Conservation Measures ECM.1, ECM.2 & ECM.3 and Building Renewal Measure BRM.1, BRM.2 & BRM.4 in Energy Audit Report
[f]Energy Conservation Measures ECM.4 & ECM.7 in Energy Audit Report
[g]Figure is calculated as the remainder of total SHARP funding after deducting funding on energy conservation measures

Table A.11 Energy consumption before and after energy retrofit works and projected savings per annum

	Pre-retrofit (2015)[a]	Post-retrofit[b]	Projected savings
Electricity			
Usage (kWh)	997,632	833,056	164,576[c]
Cost of use ($)	149,645	125,411	24,234[d]
CO_2 emission (tonnes)	50	42	8[e]
Gas			
Usage (cu.m.)	155,155	72,724	82,431[c]
Cost of use ($)	38,789	18,559	20,230[e]
CO_2 emission (tonnes)	295	138	157[e]
Total cost of use ($)	188,434	139,139	44,46[f]
Total CO_2 emission	345	180	165[c]

[a]Internat Energy Solutions (2016a), pp. 17–18
[b]Figures are calculated based on pre-retrofit and savings data
[c]Building Renewal Measure BRM.6 in Energy Audit Report
[d]Figures are calculated based on energy unit rates (Internat Energy Solutions 2016a, p. 24)
[e]Building Renewal Measure BRM.6 in Energy Audit Report
[f]Exclusive of operation savings

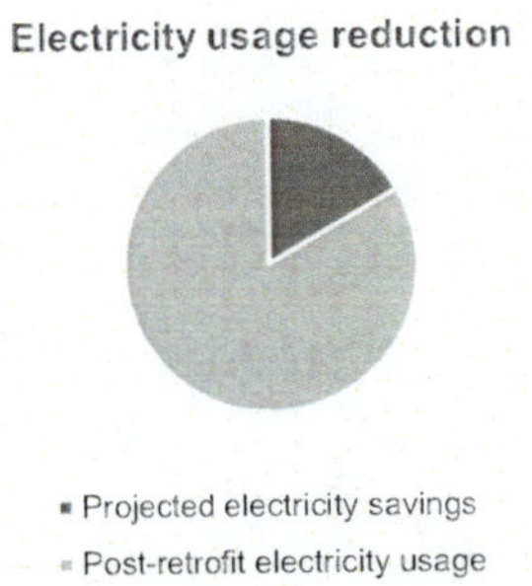

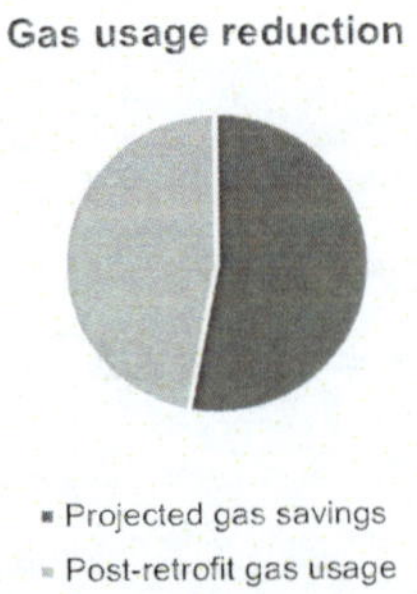

Table A.12 Cost and energy savings and anticipated payback per retrofit type

Type of retrofit	Projected annual savings[a]				Retrofit Cost[a] ($)	Anticipated simple payback[b] (years)
	Projected gas savings (m^3)	Projected electricity savings (kWh)	GHG savings (tonnes)	Cost savings ($)		
Renewable energy						
Solar wall	10,099		19	2525	53,697	21.3
Mechanical						
Heating and domestic hot water system upgrade[c]	69,983	44,127	135	28,115	713,432	25.4
Building automation system upgrade[d]	2349	2598	5	977	65,000	66.5
Non-mechanical						
Lighting retrofit[e]		117,851	6	17,678	27,858	1.6
Total	82,431	164,576	165	49,295	859,987[f]	

[a]Building Renewal Measure BRM.6 in Energy Audit Report
[b]Figures are calculated by dividing the Retrofit Cost by the Annual Cost Savings
[c]Energy Conservation Measures ECM.2 & ECM.3 in Energy Audit Report
[d]Building Renewal Measure BRM.6 in Energy Audit Report
[e]Energy Conservation Measures ECM.4 & ECM.7 in Energy Audit Report
[f]Inclusive of operation savings

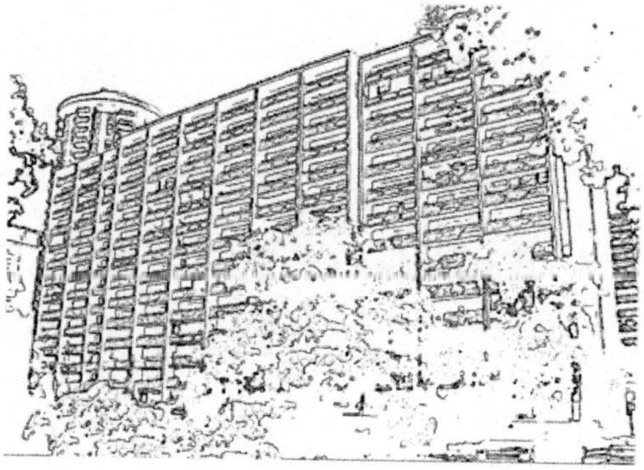

A.4 Alexander Street Project, Toronto

Table A.13 Project profile

Grant	SHARP
Development name	City Park co-operative
Address	51 Alexander street
Housing provider	City Park
Year of construction[a]	1954
Building type[b]	High-rise apartment building
Bedrooms[b]	Studio, 1–2 bedrooms
Storeys[b]	14
No. of Units[b]	256
Total funding[c]	$930,698
Program	SHARP
Funding per unit	
Rent structure	Some RGI units[d]

[a]Internat Energy Solutions (2016b), p. 4
[b]Building Renewal Measure BRM.7 in Energy Audit Report
[c]Figures are calculated based on assumption that the retrofit costs that are not covered by the incentives from utility companies are funded by the city under SHAIP
[d]51 Alexander Street is one of the three buildings within the City Park Cooperative complex with 395 RGI units

Table A.14 Energy retrofits: cost, eligible incentives from utility companies and funding received

Type of retrofit	Retrofit cost[a] ($)	Incentives[b] ($)	SHARP funding[c] ($)	% funding
Mechanical				
Heating and domestic hot water system upgrade[d]	716,405	24,584.00	691,821.00	74.3%
Building automation system upgrade[e]	65,000	–	65,000.00	7.0%
Non-mechanical				
Lighting retrofit[f]	38,528	8713.00	29,815.00	3.2%
Others				
Other costs	144,062	–	144,062.00[g]	15.5%
Total	963,995	33,297	930,698	

[a]Internat Energy Solutions (2016b), pp. 6–8
[b]Figure is calculated as the remainder of total SHARP funding after deducting funding on energy conservation measures
[c]Figures are calculated based on assumption that the retrofit costs that are not covered by the incentives from utility companies are funded by the city under SHARP
[d]Energy Conservation Measures ECM.1, ECM.2 & ECM.3 and Building Renewal Measure BRM.2, BRM.3, BRM.5 & BRM.6 in Energy Audit Report
[e]Building Renewal Measure BRM.7 in Energy Audit Report
[f]Energy Conservation Measures ECM.4, ECM.6 & ECM.7 in Energy Audit Report
[g]Figure is calculated as the remainder of total SHARP funding after deducting funding on energy conservation measures

Table A.15 Energy consumption before and after energy retrofit works and projected savings per annum

	Pre-retrofit (2015)[a]	Post-retrofit[b]	Projected savings
Electricity			
Usage (kWh)	1,008,716	833,693	175,023[c]
Cost of use ($)	151,307.0	125,053.6	26,253.38[d]
CO_2 emission (tonnes)	50	42	9[e]
Gas			
Usage (cu.m.)	155,155	82,899	72,256[c]
Cost of use ($)	38,789	20,725	18,064[e]
CO_2 emission (tonnes)	295	157	137[c]
Total cost of use ($)	190,096	145,779	44,317[f]
Total CO_2 emission	345	199	146[c]

[a]Internat Energy Solutions (2016b), pp. 17–18
[b]Figures are calculated based on pre-retrofit and savings data
[c]Figure is calculated as the remainder of total SHARP funding after deducting funding on energy conservation measures
[d]Figures are calculated based on energy unit rates (Internat Energy Solutions (2016b), p. 24)
[e]Energy Conservation Measures ECM.4, ECM.6 & ECM.7 in Energy Audit Report
[f]Exclusive of operation savings

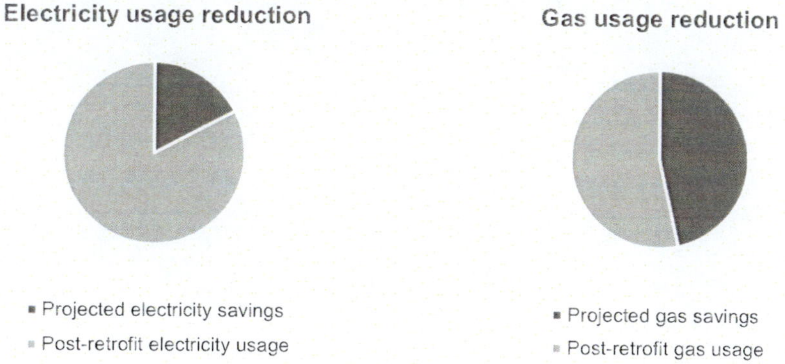

Table A.16 Cost and energy savings and anticipated payback per retrofit type

Type of retrofit	Projected annual savings[a]				Retrofit cost[a] ($)	Anticipated simple payback[b] (years)
	Projected gas savings (m^3)	Projected electricity savings (kWh)	GHG savings (tonnes)	Cost savings ($)		
Mechanical						
Heating and domestic hot water system upgrade[c]	69,907	44,127	135	28,096	716,405	25.5
Building automation system upgrade[d]	2349	2598	5	977	65,000	66.5

(continued)

Table A.16 (continued)

Type of retrofit	Projected annual savings[a]				Retrofit cost[a] ($)	Anticipated simple payback[b] (years)
	Projected gas savings (m^3)	Projected electricity savings (kWh)	GHG savings (tonnes)	Cost savings ($)		
Non-mechanical						
Lighting retrofit[e]		128,298	6	19,245	38,528	2.0
Total	72,256	175,023	146	48,318[f]		

[a]Figure is calculated as the remainder of total SHARP funding after deducting funding on energy conservation measures
[b]Figures are calculated by dividing the Retrofit Cost by the Annual Cost Savings
[c]Energy Conservation Measures ECM.1, ECM.2 & ECM.3 and Building Renewal Measure BRM.2, BRM.3, BRM.5 & BRM.6 in Energy Audit Report
[d]Building Renewal Measure BRM.7 in Energy Audit Report
[e]Energy Conservation Measures ECM.4, ECM.6 & ECM.7 in Energy Audit Report
[f]Inclusive of operation savings

A.5 Kingston Street Project, Toronto

Table A.17 Project profile

Grant	SHARP
Development name	Kingston Galloway
Address	4301 Kingston street
Housing provider	Toronto community housing corporation
Year of construction[a]	1968
Building type[b]	High-rise apartment building
Wheelchair accessibility[c]	Yes
Storeys[b]	20
No. of Units[b]	419
Total funding[d]	$4,147,960
Program	SHARP
Funding per unit	$9899.67
Rent structure[d]	410 RGI units

[a]PMC Engineering Solutions (2016), p. 8
[b]Figure is calculated as the remainder of total SHARP funding after deducting SHARP funding on energy conservation measures
[c]Toronto Community Housing Corporation (2009c)
[d]Figures are calculated based on assumption that the retrofit costs that are not covered by the incentives from utility companies are funded by the city under SHAIP

Table A.18 Types of energy retrofits: cost, eligible incentives from utility companies and funding received

Type of retrofit	Retrofit cost ($)	Incentives[a] ($)	SHARP funding ($)	Other funding sources ($)	% SHARP funding
Mechanical					
Heating and domestic hot water system upgrade	1,091,088[b]	15,824.00	847,864[c]	715,208.00[d]	20.4%
Makeup air unit upgrade	472,000[b]	3532.00			
Building automation system upgrade	20,000[b]	660.00			

(continued)

Table A.18 (continued)

Type of retrofit	Retrofit cost ($)	Incentives[a] ($)	SHARP funding ($)	Other funding sources ($)	% SHARP funding
Non-mechanical					
Window retrofit	4,860,000[b]	27,042.00	1,772,202[e]	3,060,756.00[f]	42.7%
Lighting retrofit	439,151[b]	159,893.00	207,973[e]	71,285.00[f]	5.0%
Others					
Other costs	2,669,296[g]	–	1,319,921[h]	1,349,375.00[i]	31.8%
Total	9,551,535[b]	206,951	4,147,960[j]	5,196,624[e]	

[a]PMC Engineering Solutions (2016), p. 11
[b]Figure is calculated as the sum of utility incentives, SHARP funding and other sources of funding
[c]City of Toronto's email July 17, 2019
[d]Figure is calculated as the remainder of retrofit cost after deducting utility incentives and SHARP funding
[e]City of Toronto's email July 12, 2019
[f]PMC Engineering Solutions (2016), pp. 24–25
[g]Figure is calculated as the remainder of total retrofit cost after deducting cost of energy conservation measures
[h]Figure is calculated as the remainder of total SHARP funding after deducting SHARP funding on energy conservation measures
[i]Figure is calculated as the remainder of total non-SHARP funding after deducting non-SHARP funding on energy conservation measures
[j]Prism Engineering (2016), p. 4

Table A.19 Energy consumption before and after energy retrofit works and projected savings per annum

	Pre-retrofit[a]	Post-retrofit[b]	Projected savings
Electricity			
Usage (kWh)	3,313,641	2,151,524	1,162,117[c]
Cost of use ($)	441,364	286,574	154,789[d]
CO_2 emission (tonnes)	265	172	93[e]
Gas			
Usage (cu.m.)	535,876	420,238	115,638[c]
Cost of use ($)	181,134	142,046	39,087[e]
CO_2 emission (tonnes)	1012	793	218[e]
Total cost of use ($)	2,265,725	2,071,850	193,876[c]
Total CO_2 emission	2,888,222	2,887,912	311[c]

[a]PMC Engineering Solutions (2016), pp. 24–25
[b]Figures are calculated based on pre-retrofit and savings data.
[c]Prism Engineering (2016), p. 3
[d]Figures are calculated based on energy unit rates (PMC Engineering Solutions (2016), p. 24)
[e]Prism Engineering (2016), p. 6

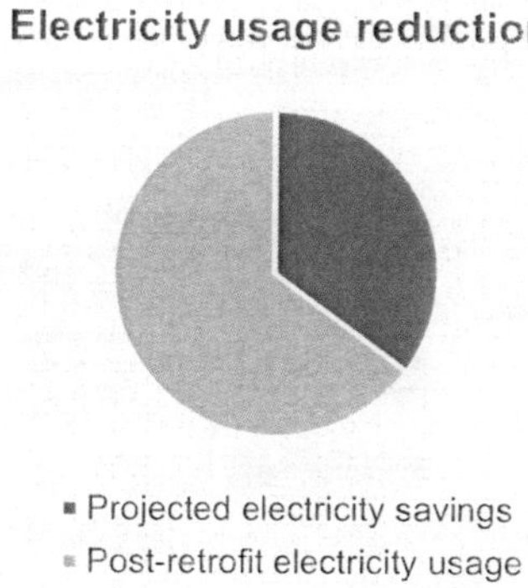

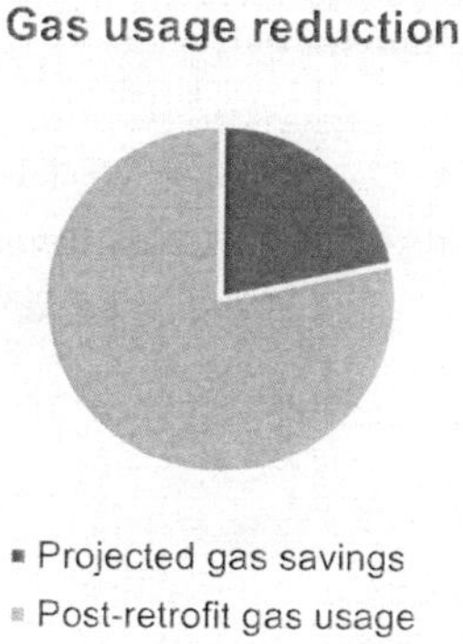

Table A.20 Costs and energy savings and anticipated payback per retrofit type

Type of retrofit	Projected annual savings[a]				Retrofit Cost[a]	Anticipated simple payback[b] (years)
	Projected gas savings (m^3)	Projected electricity savings (kWh)	GHG savings (tonnes)	Cost savings		
Mechanical						
Heating and domestic hot water system upgrade	38,338	119,900	82	28,929	1,091,088	37.7
Makeup air unit upgrade	10,185	25,130	21	6790	472,000	69.5
Building automation system upgrade	1597	4996	3	1205	20,000	16.6
Non-mechanical						
Window retrofit	65,517	204,899	140	49,437	4,860,000	98.3
Lighting retrofit	–	807,192	64.71	107,514.67	439,151	4.1
Total	115,638	1,162,117	311	193,876	6,882,239	

[a]Figure is calculated as the sum of utility incentives, SHARP funding and other sources of funding
[b]Figures are calculated by dividing the Retrofit Cost by the Annual Cost Savings

A.6 Grandview Terrace Project, Vancouver

Table A.21 Project profile

Grant	
Development name	Grandview terrace
Address	1441 Graveley St, Vancouver
Housing provider	BC housing[a]
Year of construction[b]	1967
Building type[c]	Highrise apartments + townhouses
Bedrooms[c]	Studios +1-2-3 bedrooms
Storeys[c]	Up to 5 storeys
No. of Units[c]	154

[a]BC Housing (n.d.)
[b]Prism Engineering (2016), p. 4
[c]Exclusive of operation savings

Table A.22 Energy retrofits: cost, eligible incentives from utility companies and funding received

Type of retrofit	Retrofit cost ($)	Incentives[a] ($)	Funding ($)	% funding
Mechanical				
Heating and DHW system upgrade	27,700[b]	–	27,700.00	
Non-mechanical				
Bathroom retrofit	24,000[b]	–	24,000.00	
Window/door retrofit	175,700[c]	–	175,700.00	
Lighting retrofit	56,100[b]	4700.00	51,400.00	
Wall insulation	267,500[d]	–	267,500.00	
Others				
Other costs		–		
Total		4700		

[a]Prism Engineering (2016), p. 3
[b]Figures are calculated by dividing the Retrofit Cost by the Annual Cost Savings
[c]Average capital repair cost (Prism Engineering 2016, p. 29)
[d]Energy Savings Measures 5.3 & 5.5 in Energy Audit Report

Table A.23 Energy consumption before and after energy retrofit works and projected savings per annum

2015	Pre-retrofit[a]	Post-retrofit[b]	Projected savings
Electricity			
Usage (kWh)	146,842.0	109,962.0	36,880.0[c]
Cost of use ($)	15,795.0	11,828.0	3967.0[d]
CO2 emission (tonnes)	1.6	1.2	0.4[e]
Gas			
Usage (cu.m.)	189,206.2	139,098.5	50,107.7[c]
Cost of use ($)	10,497.0	7717.1	2779.9[e]
CO_2 emission (tonnes)	351.3	258.3	93.0[c]
Total cost of use ($)	26,292.0	19,545.1	6746.9[f]
Total CO_2 emission	353.0	259.6	93.4[c]

[a]Prism Engineering (2016), p. 6
[b]Figures are calculated based on pre-retrofit and savings data
[c]Figures are calculated by dividing the Retrofit Cost by the Annual Cost Savings
[d]Prism Engineering (2016), p. 5 & Prism Engineering (2016), Appendix C
[e]Energy Savings Measures 5.1 & 5.2 in Energy Audit Report
[f]Exclusive of operation savings

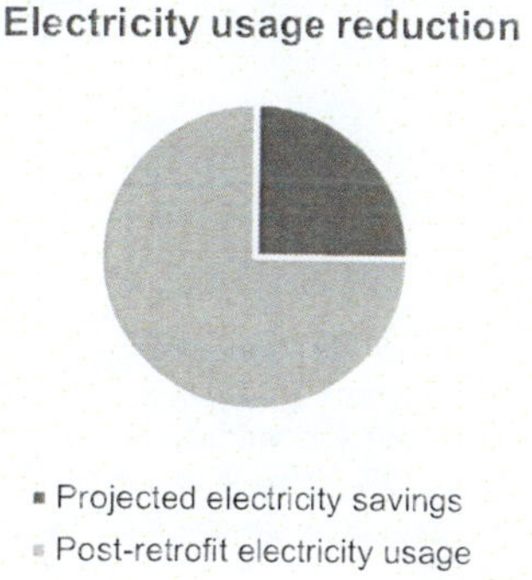

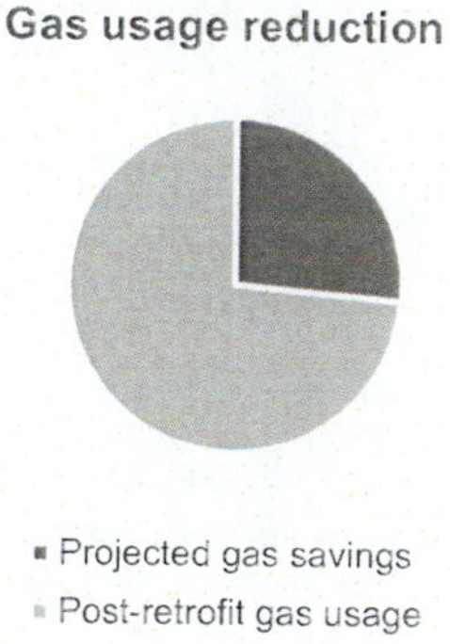

Table A.24 Projected cost and energy savings and anticipated payback per retrofit type

Type of retrofit	Projected annual savings[a]				Retrofit cost[a] ($)	Anticipated simple payback[a] (years)
	Projected gas savings (m^3)	Projected elect savings (kWh)	GHG savings (tonnes)	Cost savings ($)		
Mechanical						
Heating and domestic hot water system upgrade[b]	1423.21	10,200.00	2.70	1350.00	27,700.00	20.5

(continued)

Table A.24 (continued)

Type of retrofit	Projected annual savings[a]				Retrofit cost[a] ($)	Anticipated simple payback[a] (years)
	Projected gas savings (m^3)	Projected elect savings (kWh)	GHG savings (tonnes)	Cost savings ($)		
Non-mechanical						
Bathroom retrofit[c]	20,300.87		37.70	6450.00	24,000.00	3.7
Window/door retrofit[d]	28,383.62		52.70	9010.00	175,700.00	19.5
Lighting retrofit[e]		26,680.00	0.30	5560.00	56,100.00	10.1
Wall insulation[f]	7518.84		14.00	2390.00	267,500.00	111.9
Total	50,107.70	36,880.00	93.40	24,760.00[g]		

[a]Figures are calculated by dividing the Retrofit Cost by the Annual Cost Savings
[b]Energy Savings Measures 5.3 & 5.5 in Energy Audit Report
[c]Energy Savings Measure 5.13 in Energy Audit Report
[d]Energy Savings Measure 5.12 and Capital Upgrade 6.4 in Energy Audit Report
[e]Energy Savings Measures 5.1 & 5.2 in Energy Audit Report
[f]Capital Upgrade 6.5 in Energy Audit Report
[g]Inclusive of operation savings

References

BC Housing. (n.d.). *Directly Managed Properties*. Retrieved from BC Housing: https://www.bchousing.org/housing-assistance/tenant-programs-resources/directly-managed-properties

Internat Energy Solutions. (2016a). *Energy Assessment Report: City Park Cooperative 484 Church St., Toronto, Ontario.* Toronto, ON: Internat Energy Solutions Canada Inc.

Internat Energy Solutions. (2016b). *Energy Assessment Report: City Park Cooperative 51 Alexander St., Toronto, Ontario.* Toronto, ON: Internat Energy Solutions Canada Inc.

PMC Engineering Services. (2018). *Energy Audit Report - 40 Falstaff Ave, North York, Ontario.* PMC Engineering Services.

PMC Engineering Solutions. (2016). *Energy Audit Report - 4301 Kingston Road, Scarborough, ON.* Toronto, ON: PMC Engineering Solutions.

PMC Engineering Solutions. (2018). *Energy Audit Report - 6 Glamorgan Ave, Scarborough, ON.* PMC Engineering Solutions.

Prism Engineering. (2016). *Detailed Energy Audit Report - Grandview Terrace 1441 Graveley St, Vancouver.* Burnaby, BC: Prism Engineering.

Toronto Community Housing Corporation. (2009a). *Northeast - Family Housing - 3 Bedroom Units.* Retrieved from https://www.torontohousing.ca/residents/your-tenancy/Documents/NORTHEAST%20FAMILY%203-BED%20UNITS%20MAP%20and%20LIST%202,011.pdf

Toronto Community Housing Corporation. (2009b). *Northwest - Family Housing - 1 Bedroom Units.* Retrieved from https://www.torontohousing.ca/residents/your-tenancy/Documents/NORTHWEST%20FAMILY%201-BED%20UNITS%20MAP%20and%20LIST%202,011.pdf

Toronto Community Housing Corporation. (2009c). *Northeast - Family Housing - 2 Bedroom Units.* Retrieved from https://www.torontohousing.ca/residents/your-tenancy/Documents/NORTHEAST%20FAMILY%202-BED%20UNITS%20MAP%20and%20LIST%202,011.pdf